MONTESSORI AT HOME

MONTESSORI AT HOME

A Practical Guide for Parents

From Birth to Age 3

Tara Greaney

ROCKRIDGE
PRESS

To all the parents at Caedmon School,
Cravath's Christine Beshar Children's Center,
and Morningside Montessori School
who shared their children with me over the
past 45 years. Your children have
taught me much and truly enriched my life.
Thank you.

Contents

Introduction

My passion for teaching young children started with a love of dolls, babies, and little kids. As the oldest sibling with a network of 20 younger cousins, I built a reputation as the town babysitter, especially for large families. My Irish immigrant family cherished education and built into all of us "Faghliam an tSaoil," the belief in lifelong learning. Sunup to sundown, birth to death, learn something new every day.

By the time I got to college and discovered a new Montessori training program, I was hooked on early childhood education. After graduation, I joined Caedmon School, the first Montessori school in New York City. There, under Douglas Gravel, head of school, and Carol Devine, my head teacher at the time who later became head of school, I learned how to be a Montessorian in class and in life. The next 50 years (49, but who's counting?) have given me joy every day.

Today there are thousands of Montessori schools worldwide. There are public, private, and charter Montessori schools that serve children from birth through high school in more than 110 countries. In the United States the majority of children who attend Montessori schools do so at the preschool level, which is designed for children aged three to six.

What's unique about Montessori is that it truly respects the child's choices and allows each individual to grow to their fullest potential, whatever that might be. The school encourages children—even those with various special needs—to develop confidence and independence by carefully looking at, assessing, and designing their environment. A prepared environment allows the child to make choices. Children are awarded time to observe, reflect, engage, plan, think, and absorb what is going on so they can successfully navigate their world.

Montessori believes that any parent, family member, teacher, and caregiver in a child's life can be the "guide," but with training. They're charged with observing the child at different developmental stages to see if they're ready to move on to the next challenge. Unlike the traditional school that I, and maybe you, attended, Montessori uses didactic materials to teach. Children learn basic math by using counters. Reading preparation begins by touching and tracing sandpaper letters. Giving young children the opportunity to manipulate materials enables them to understand concepts, self-correct, and love learning. Throughout all of this, Montessori follows the child. By observing the child, the guide is able to present what the child is ready for and can accomplish successfully. That is the foundation for building their self-esteem and confidence.

This is my passion and why I still train Montessori infant/toddler teachers and hold workshops. I am thrilled that you picked up this book, I wrote it for you, parents who want to embrace the Montessori way in their own home. My hope is to give you a broad under-standing of the founder, Maria Montessori; who she was, and how she influenced millions of children's lives all over the world.

In this book, you'll find chapters that focus on the first six years of your child's life. I address developmental milestones and issues for each age range. I also provide clear and useful guidelines on how to prepare your home so that you can offer the best practices in raising your child within the Montessori philosophy.

Inside, you'll find useful and important games and exercises for you to engage in with your child, each earmarked for a specific age and modified to meet the development goals. These chapters will take you from the first few months of parenthood to that milestone first birthday. As your child ages, the tips and suggestions for changing the physical space in your home, the pedagogy you use, and the behaviors you will observe will change. I will continue through the chapters until your child is six, enters a new plane of development, and is off to kindergarten.

At each stage I will offer ideas for observing sensitive periods, preparing the environment, and presenting opportunities to enhance the sensorial, math, language, social, and emotional development of your child. You can use some or many of the suggestions. Remember to enjoy your child first and foremost.

Part 1

The Parent's Guide to Montessori

In part 1, you'll learn the basic tenets of the Montessori method—and why it continues to be such a popular form of interacting with children all around the world. Armed with a greater understanding of the philosophy and instruction style, referred to as pedagogy, you'll be more equipped to integrate it into your home, and your child's life, in part 2.

Montessori 101

Welcome to the world of Montessori. In this chapter, you'll discover the core concepts of Montessori's method for providing children with their physical, social, emotional, cognitive, and moral development. This will give you the crucial context needed to make the most of the practical advice throughout the rest of the book.

Why Montessori?

Whether you plan to send your child to a Montessori school or traditional preschool, there are many ways to incorporate Montessori's concepts into your everyday life. From infancy on, your child is absorbing everything about the world around them through all of their senses. The founder, Maria Montessori called this "the absorbent mind." She stressed the importance of preparing the environment that your child is in, being mindful of all that they may absorb, respecting your child, and providing freedom but having limits. By objectively observing your child, you can follow their lead and prepare tweaks to your home that allow them to develop their potential.

A SENSE OF INDEPENDENCE. Montessori allows a child to make choices, learn, and practice how to take care of themselves and their environment, fostering a willingness to explore and an eagerness to pursue learning.

GRACE AND COURTESY. Montessori shows children how to act with and treat one another. Children are encouraged to be sensitive to one another's feelings, develop empathy, and learn appropriate words to use with other children and adults.

A LOVE OF LEARNING. With the Montessori method, every day is an adventure in the acquisition of knowledge, instilling a love of learning in children from a young age.

CONFIDENCE. Children placed in an environment that enables them to make choices, given materials they are successful with, and surrounded by adults who respect them. It's only natural for your child to grow more confident from a young age.

HIGH SELF-ESTEEM. A child's self-esteem begins at birth. It develops and grows through successful social interactions and Montessori is cognizant of these. When you show respect for a child from birth on, their unconscious absorbent mind internalizes it, and the seeds of self-esteem are planted.

AN ABILITY TO RESOLVE CONFLICT. Maria Montessori lived through two world wars and was very cognizant of the need for peace and social justice. The Montessori method asks children to set the guidelines for how they would like to be treated, and to agree that everyone in the classroom will abide by the same rules. When children disagree, they are encouraged to go to a "peace table," discuss their differences, and resolve them. In the process, they learn that differences are natural.

A DESIRE TO BE ORGANIZED. The Montessori method facilitates a child's natural tendency toward order (see page 14), so they feel good organizing their belongings and being in greater control over their environment. This benefit proves particularly useful at home.

SENSE OF WONDER. Let your child be your guide through their discovery of new experiences, objects, and activities. Share in that wonder: Stop and look at life through the eyes of your child. Ask them lots of questions: Why does the dog wag his tail? Do you think the soap will sink or float in the tub? Why? How are cookies made? The more you facilitate your child's sense of wonder, the more joy you'll experience while parenting.

Nobody Solves a Problem Like Maria

Today, there are thousands of Montessori schools around the world, responsible for serving millions of children. None of them would exist, of course, were it not for the incredible ingenuity and determination of Maria Montessori herself.

Born in 1870, Montessori came from the working-class town of Chiaravalle in Italy. Unlike most women around the world, those in Chiaravalle had the opportunity to accrue wealth and power. They formed labor collaborations, resulting in improvements for the workers and their families. Clearly, this made an impression on young Maria.

When Maria was six, her family moved to Rome. At the age of 13, she persuaded her parents to let her attend a predominantly male school; more impressive still, at 20, she enrolled in the University of Rome. While studying to become a doctor, she spent time in the asylums of children deemed mentally ill or developmentally challenged. Her interest in the French physicians Jean Marc Gaspard Itard, known mostly for his work with deaf students, and Edouard Séguin, renowned for his work with the intellectually disabled, led her to focus on how children developed (or did not develop) cognitively, socially, and emotionally.

When Maria was 29, she further upended the norms of the day, giving birth to a son, Mario, out of wedlock. In the face of adversity, she became an outspoken advocate for women's education and equal pay. She was appointed Director of Rome's Orthophrenic School, where she trained teachers to work with children deemed mentally ill or developmentally challenged.

In 1907, she was asked to oversee a new preschool for disadvantaged three- to six-year-old children in a low-income area of Rome, called Casa dei Bambini (House of Children). This was where Maria practiced the unique pedagogy her eponymous institutions still embrace today. The school encouraged children to learn through their senses, move at their own pace, freely explore a prepared environment, develop a strong sense of independence, and more. In 1909, she published *The Montessori Method*, which has been translated into 10 languages.

She went on to open two more Casa dei Bambini schools, eventually expanding her purview to include elementary school–age children. By 1920, Maria was researching adolescents and training teachers—known as "guides"—to work with the children.

Maria traveled to Argentina, Ireland, Germany, India, Pakistan, Sweden, Sri Lanka and more, to lecture, write, and establish training programs for Montessori schools that opened all around the world. The first Montessori school to open in the United States, in 1911, was located in Scarborough, New York. By 1916, more than 100 Montessori schools had opened in the United States.

Interest in Montessori began to fade by World War I, but Maria soldiered on. In 1929, she and her son established the Association Montessori International. She went on to write numerous books and was nominated for the Nobel Peace Prize in 1949, 1950, and 1951. Maria died in 1952, but her legacy lives on. In the 1950s and 1960s, interest in Montessori schools started to increase again, and by 1960 the American Montessori Society was established. Today there are approximately 5,000 Montessori schools in the United States.

Montessori's Core Concepts

Montessori's philosophy is rooted in seven core concepts. These concepts will serve as the foundation for the more specific advice on pedagogy and instruction delivered in part 2.

THE ABSORBENT MIND

The things he sees are not just remembered;
they form a part of his soul.

— The Absorbent Mind

Montessori believed that children from birth to age three have an *unconscious absorbent mind*. They take in a wealth of information about the world through their senses—the first tools a child knows how to use—and formulate foundational ideas about their environment that they will call upon later in life. From age three on, Montessori believed, children have a *conscious absorbent mind*, at which point they seek out new information more intentionally. An infant unconsciously absorbs the language spoken in their home; a four-year-old consciously wants to be able to learn to read.

Providing opportunities for your child to refine and experience their senses of touch, taste, smell, sight, and sound is paramount during these first few years. Talk to them before they are able to talk; share your passions. They will pick up the excitement in your voice and join you in your hobby. Taking your child with you on nature walks can help pique their curiosity about the natural world. A trip to the art museum can help build a foundation for their appreciation for the arts. Infants and toddlers absorb not only the physical things they see, hear, and touch, but also your enthusiasm.

OBSERVATION

The child's way of doing things has been for us an inexhaustible fountain of revelations.

— The Absorbent Mind

By observing a child, Montessori could understand the sort of information and experiences they were unconsciously absorbing in their environment, as well as the cause and effect of various factors.

As a parent, you have an incredibly personal relationship with your child. Learning to keep your observations more objective is critical to the development of your child. By stepping back and watching, you'll be prepared to follow your child's lead and adjust their environment accordingly.

PREPARED ENVIRONMENT

The first aim of the prepared environment is, as far as it is possible, to render the growing child independent of the adult.

— The Secret of Childhood

Through observation, Montessori realized the extent of a child's capacity to absorb information about their world and store it in their memory bank. Naturally, she designed an environment for the children that would enhance this capacity. There are three main components of a Montessori environment: the room and furniture arrangement, the materials present, and the adult guides (or parents) who observe the child and guide them toward prepared activities.

The classroom, or in your case, your home, should provide freedom for the child to move around, socialize, and make simple choices. Everything should be in sight and reach of the child. Your home should be clean, orderly, and full of natural materials and plants, making it a healthy, peaceful place to work for both children and adults. (In the next chapter, we'll go over how to ensure your home incorporates these Montessori traits.)

FREEDOM WITH LIMITS

Little children, from the moment they are weaned, are making their way toward independence.

— The Montessori Reader

Montessori believed children need to have freedom to explore their environment from the time they are born. But with freedom comes some necessary limits. The parent or guide is responsible for preparing the environment—not only for a child's safety but also to provide the sense of security that comes with boundaries.

As you'll discover in part 2, movement is particularly important. Infants should be placed on various textures, so they can touch and explore. As the child begins to walk, the environment will need to include more toys and activities with which to engage. As children get older, it's a good idea to give them the freedom to make choices within the limits you've defined. Such freedom will boost their self-esteem and independence.

LET THE CHILD LEAD

An adult can assist in shaping the environment but it is the child that perfects his own being.

— The Secret of Childhood

As Montessori parents, you will discover that you cannot force your child to see wonder. Learn to respect and accept the choices that your child makes. They may show a preference for numbers, bugs, music, stories, or dancing. They will repeatedly engage in these activities, perfecting them.

Take note of whatever interests them and do your best to nurture those interests with new materials and experiences. Enjoy seeing the world through their eyes.

INDEPENDENCE

> *The environment must be rich in motives which lend interest to activity and invite the child to conduct his own experiences.*
>
> — Dr. Montessori's
> Own Handbook

As infants and toddlers, children's freedom in prepared environments gives them the independence they need to move about, make choices, and take care of themselves. As they grow, it also enhances their willingness to search for information and knowledge. Without a sense of independence, children will not be as inclined to explore and discover new people, cultures, experiences, places, and materials, nor will they have the confidence to express themselves creatively.

RESPECT FOR THE CHILD

> *Children are human beings to whom respect is due, superior to us by reason of their innocence and the greater possibilities of their future.*
>
> — Dr. Montessori's
> Own Handbook

On a practical level, this means showing your children they are worthy of your time and attention. Take your time, give them your undivided attention, and enjoy each stage that they move through. This respect will help boost their confidence, self-esteem, and willingness to explore—all of which are key to the development of their full potential.

Of course, respect also means treating them as those "to whom respect is due"—rather than mere children whose feelings are not taken seriously. For example, if a toddler falls and scrapes their knee, many parents would try to comfort them by saying, "Don't worry, you're okay." Though well-intentioned, a better idea would be to acknowledge their hurt and assure them that there will be an end to their pain: "I know your knee hurts. It will probably hurt until dinnertime, but then it will feel better." This is how their resilience starts to develop.

What You Need to Know About "Sensitive Periods"

Montessori's theory of human development from birth to age 24 provides a holistic framework that encompasses the whole person— their cognitive, spiritual, moral, emotional, social, and physical development. She divides human growth into four "planes," each of which lasts about six years: infancy (physical independence), childhood (mental independence), adolescence (social independence), and maturity (spiritual and moral independence).

In the first plane, Montessori points out various "sensitive periods"— times in which children are more receptive to and interested in different skills. During these times, children are more willing to practice, and eventually master, these skills. Sensitive periods last as long as is necessary for the child to continue to engage in them. They are not critical or fixed periods that have fixed onsets and terminations.

In the following chart, I've identified the sensitive periods for a child's first plane of development—in other words, their first six years. You'll want to keep these in mind as you go about preparing your home for your child.

SENSITIVE PERIOD	AGE RANGE	DESCRIPTION
Language (Nonverbal Communication)	Birth through 7 months	They make sounds and gestures to see what works for them.
Language (Verbal Communication)	7 months to 3 years	They remember certain sounds are associated with certain consequences. One-word sentences and two-word combinations; grammar and syntax soon follow.
Language (Various Forms of Communicating)	2½ to 5 years	They know letters represent sounds and sounds make words.
Language (Reading)	3½ to 4½ years	They put letters together to read phonetic words.
Language (Reading and Writing)	4½ to 6 years	They're beginning to read and show an interest in writing words.
Order	Birth through 12 months	They recognize things they've seen, heard, touched, tasted, or smelled.
Order	12 months to 3½ years	They're cognizant of the order of small objects.
Movement	Birth through 2 years	Infants learn to operate their bodies; they roll over, sit up, crawl, and pull themselves up; around 12 months they cruise around and eventually let go and walk.

SENSITIVE PERIOD	AGE RANGE	DESCRIPTION
Movement	2½ to 6 years	They walk on their own for significant distances. Small and large muscle coordination is also refined.
Toileting	1 to 3 years, depending on culture	They show interest in what goes in and comes out of their bodies.
Grace and Courtesy	2½ to 6 years	They learn to speak to and communicate with one another and show compassion and empathy toward one another.
Small Objects	12 months to 6 years	They develop attention to detail and are fascinated by small objects.
Music	2 to 6 years	They show interest in rhythm, rhymes, pitch, and melody.
Refinement of Senses	Birth to 2 years	They express their likes and dislikes of what they encounter through gestures and sounds.
Refinement of Senses	2 to 6 years	They use words and all of their senses to make assumptions about their world.

Montessori's Behavioral Tendencies

Integral to Montessori's philosophy was her belief, grounded in decades of research, that all children are born with tendencies—natural predispositions to think or behave in certain ways. She identified 11 in total.

ORIENTATION

From birth on, children like to know where they are. Infants draw on all of their senses to orient themselves. They look, listen, and smell to pick up on the scent of their mother and make emotional connections through touch. Toddlers, who are more independent, like to know where objects are located and where they themselves fit into a given situation. Two-year-olds like to know where they play, eat, sleep, and sometimes the route to Grandma's house or the food store. They want to know where they are in relationship to the world around them.

As we discussed earlier in the chapter, it's important to be mindful of your child's environment. Children are comforted by their knowledge of where the couch or bookshelf is in their home; changing furniture around can be upsetting. When your child is a baby, orient them through talk. Tell them what you are doing, where you are going, when they will be tended to. Even if they cannot understand the words, they like the sound of your voice, its tone, and its volume. Your voice lets them know they are in a safe, familiar place. Eventually, they will get to know your routines and understand your explanations. They are absorbing much more than you may realize.

ORDER

Somewhat related to orientation, all children yearn for a sense of security. An orderly environment is more predictable than a chaotic one and therefore is much more secure. Children love to know where certain objects belong; putting them there can contribute to a sense of calm. Do your best to show children where things are located, particularly items they'll use, such as clothes and toys. Routines give children a sense of order, as they can predict what will happen next. After a bath is a story, then bedtime. External order leads to internal order.

EXPLORATION

Children are born with a quest to learn about and understand the world around them—a sense of wonder about discovering novel things. Starting in infancy, you'll want to nourish this tendency by surrounding your child with safe and beautiful textures, sounds, scents, colors, and objects; anything in sight should be available for them to reach and touch. An environment in which objects that a child approaches are moved beyond reach can be very discouraging. You'll want to give your infant the freedom to move in a safe space where they can roll over, worm around, crawl, and eventually pull themselves up before walking.

COMMUNICATION

Humans are born with the desire to communicate. We strive to understand and be understood. Infants start off communicating to the outside world by making sounds (e.g., crying) to communicate that they are hungry, tired, soiled, or bored. They use gestures—throwing their arms up, turning their heads this way or that, and the like—to communicate other feelings. Eventually, they learn that certain sounds are associated with what they want or need: "Mama" gets the attention of their mother; "cookie" gets them a treat.

Communication is a key part of creating your prepared environment (see page 44). Be sure to describe, in words, the objects you've placed in the environment. Explain to your child that their blanket, for example, is soft, or that their oatmeal is warm. Use books to provide them with vocabulary words that don't pop up in everyday conversation at home. Books filled with realistic photos of everyday items is a great place to start. A photo album with pictures of your family members, including the pets is another great approach.

ACTIVITY

One of the core Montessori ideas is that children learn by doing—and that they learn even better if they can teach what they learned to someone else. For example, you will often see a four-year-old child help a younger sibling or classmate button or zip up their jacket. As is the case for adults, a child's ability to absorb cognitive information is improved when they are physically active. One simple example of this is counting to five as your child stacks blocks. The activity of stacking the blocks helps solidify the skill of rote counting and eventually develops one-to-one correspondence. (You'll find many activities like this in part 2.)

MANIPULATION

Children need to touch their environment to understand it. This is especially true when children are young. Older children can rely more on cognitive concepts, but before age six, manipulation is best. If they can feel the texture, weight, or temperature of an object, more information is going to the brain. Children who can manipulate one block and compare it with 10 blocks can feel and see the differences. Indeed, humans "manipulated" objects to create the first tools many ages ago.

WORK

Everyone has work to do. This was true in Montessori's time, and it's certainly still the case today. A child's work is to play. Playing is, quite simply, what they are meant to be doing. Moving about, handling different objects, making small yet significant discoveries—all are part of a child's work. Montessori believed that through this work, children develop a sense of accomplishment, self-esteem, and understanding of themselves.

Their quest for independence will make them want to do the same things that you're doing around the house. Let them join you in your tasks and find age-appropriate activities they can do. One-year-olds can pick up toys and put them in a basket. Two-year-olds can sort their clean laundry into different piles. Three-year-olds love to help wipe the table, sweep the floor, and even pull weeds! (You can find many more examples of age-appropriate activities in part 2.)

REPETITION

Children will repeat activities over and over until they master them. This gives them a great sense of accomplishment. And after they've mastered the activity, a child will often continue to repeat it out of sheer pleasure. Even infants learn that if they kick an activity bar with their foot, it makes a sound—and they'll repeat this over and over. Toddlers may ask you to read a book again and again (and again). This repetition sharpens their memory and gives them comfort in knowing what's coming next.

EXACTNESS

As you'll discover later in the book, Montessori materials are designed to have only one correct solution, so a child knows right away if, say, the puzzle piece fits or not. This feeds into their inclination toward exactness—a predictable and orderly sense of stability, which is quite satisfying.

ABSTRACTION

At first, children learn the names of objects in their world: ball, doll, dog, block, bottle. As they grow, they have a tendency to think more abstractly about objects. A branch can become a flag, a blanket can become a cape. Abstraction shows a higher level of cognitive functioning, bolstering a child's creativity and imagination.

PERFECTION

As humans, we love to get everything right—be it a poem, a song, a dance, a relationship, a puzzle, or a recipe. This starts at birth. With repetition, children continue to develop a skill to the point of mastery. So, if your child is determined to scoop up that last pea with their spoon, let them. The sense of accomplishment that comes with perfecting a task contributes to their self-esteem and confidence.

The Modern Montessori School

It wasn't until the 1960s that Montessori schools really took off in the United States. The culture was changing. More and more mothers were entering the workforce. As educators realized all children younger than six require some form of education, childcare and preschool became interchangeable. *Sesame Street*, nationwide Head Start programs, and even the 1957 launch of Sputnik all spurred interest in early childhood education. Most critical, perhaps, was the desire for progressive schools with innovative programs—including the Montessori method.

Montessori programs also contributed to the desegregation efforts of the 1960s. As an article in the Fall 2020 issue of *Montessori Life* noted, "Many private schools followed the public school's lead in terms of integration, and this led many Montessori schools to announce a commitment to racial and ethnic diversity and social justice."

Today there are approximately 5,000 Montessori schools in the United States. This is in addition to hundreds of training programs and a proliferation of organizations, blogs, and online resources, according to the American Montessori Society. While only about 500 of the 5,000 Montessori programs are public, approximately 300 of those public programs were added in the last 20 years, according to data from the National Center for Montessori in the Public Sector.

Many Montessori schools accept children as young as two months old; some continue to educate children through high school. Most programs, however, are designed for preschool-aged children.

In the past, Montessori was often maligned as a school for the well-off, but today, Montessori schools do make an effort to enroll lower-income families. Many are not-for-profit and most provide financial aid.

I am head of a Montessori school in New York City that has been open since 1964. We have a specially designed environment and pedagogy for our two-year-olds program. Our early-childhood program (ages three to six) incorporates English, Mandarin, Spanish, and French, as well as music, movement, swimming, cooking, and sewing. Our children arrive between 8 and 9 a.m. and stay until 12:30, 3:30, or 6 p.m., depending on their parents' schedules. Like all Montessori classrooms, ours is designed with areas for practical life activities, sensorial activities, math, language, art, blocks, geography, food preparation, and plenty of outdoor playground space.

Montessori schools in different locations incorporate their larger environment—be they farms, forests, seasides, or inner cities—into the learning environment of the child.

What's the Difference Between a Traditional Preschool and a Montessori Preschool?

Traditional preschools and Montessori preschools have much in common. They provide an ample opportunity for children to socialize, play, and learn the fundamentals of pre-reading and pre-math from nurturing adults, as well as to read books and interact with child-size furniture. Yet, as illustrated in the table that follows, there are several key differences.

Educational Approach	TRADITIONAL PRESCHOOLS	MONTESSORI PRESCHOOLS
Curriculum	• Have a set curriculum • In many non-Montessori schools, children all do the same work at the same time, regardless of what level they're at individually • Group snack and a group circle time	• Each child is observed daily and records are used to determine what they might be interested in or ready to discover • Teacher/guide introduces the child to new material or experience individually or in a small group • Children are encouraged to find the wonder in the room and spend time observing and engaging in activities
Room Design	• Set up with areas for art, pretend play, blocks, and tables that can accommodate a group of children • Children's work is displayed at all levels around the room	• Classrooms are full of natural materials, photos, and books with realistic pictures • Layout flows like a home: entrance; bathroom; kitchen/food preparation area; resting/sleeping section; outdoor area; and a living/work space, where materials are available • Also, there are distinct spaces for practical life, sensorial, math, and language materials and activities

Educational Approach	TRADITIONAL PRESCHOOLS	MONTESSORI PRESCHOOLS
Teachers	• Teachers have certain degrees and certifications (depending on regional licensing requirements) • Staffing is goverened by state or national codes usually with a ratio of one adult per 10 to 12 children	• Must meet regional codes for ratios and certification • Montessori teacher certification is also required (takes one or two years of training)
Independence	• Children are prepared for kindergarten and traditional elementary school, where they will line up for activities, listen quietly to lectures, and take standardized tests	• Children are taught to be mindful of and to express their feelings • Children learn to expect that they will be acknowledged and responded to—as a result, they become more independent and confident as they master different tasks

Montessori at Home

Now that you have a greater understanding of Montessori's teachings of the absorbent mind, the importance of observation to follow the child's lead, and respect for your child's interests and abilities, we can start to implement Montessori ideas into your home to enhance your child's development. In this chapter, we'll focus on preparing yourself, preparing the environment (your home), gathering the right materials, and safety. Once you understand the basic tenets of a Montessori home, it will be easy (and fun) to create your own.

Implementing the Montessori Method

As you discovered in chapter 1, Maria Montessori designed her first school to be a homelike place where students could develop independence, self-esteem, and practical life skills. In many ways, then, your home is already designed to incorporate Montessori's core ideas.

The prepared environment, which was important to Maria Montessori because it is where the child spends their day, has three components.

THE SPACE ITSELF. You may start with one area, such as your child's room and then add on more as you become more comfortable with the concept and as your child grows. The area should foster independence and exploration while allowing freedom of movement within clear limits.

MATERIALS MATTER. The items that you put in your prepared environment should invite wonder and curiosity. They should call out for your child to touch and engage. For example, a wristband on your infant that rattles whenever they move their arm, a basket of balls for your one-year-old, or a bowl full of slime for a two-year-old.

THE ADULTS IN THE ROOM. This could be the parents, caregivers, and/or other adults in the home. These adults should have a basic understanding of the Montessori approach.

Preparing the Adult (That's You!)

The real preparation for education is a study of one's self. The training of the teacher . . . is something far more than a learning of ideas. It includes the training of character; it is a preparation of the spirit.

— The Absorbent Mind

Montessori created a methodology for teachers that allows children to develop independence, confidence, and a love of learning. The primary role of a parent or caregiver is to help the child reach their maximum potential. However, it is not necessarily your job to define what, exactly, their "maximum potential" means.

The same can be said for the personality, temperament, and passion that your child exhibits. It may be hard for a reserved parent to have a child whose dream is to sing songs to strangers, or for an athletic parent to have a child with no interest in sports. But Montessori was about accepting children as they are.

It is important to understand that children grow and go through stages. Their parents do, as well, as they nurture and guide their children before eventually letting them go. Preparing to parent a child through the lens of Montessori philosophy may require some reevaluations of long-held beliefs. To help you in this process, I offer you some thought-provoking questions to ask yourself and the others who will be partnering with you to raise your child.

Montessori believed that adults who interact with a child on a daily basis—guides, parents or childcare providers—should:

- Have a basic knowledge of child development and the absorbent minds of children

- Be keen observers and objective recorders of children and their environments

- Be able to follow the child's lead and interests

- Prepare an environment full of wonder that fosters independence and freedom with limits

- Understand health and safety training for children

The following is a parental "to-do" list, with pointers and tips for you to keep in mind as you move through the book.

ENGAGE IN SELF-REFLECTION. Ask yourself what really makes you happy/sad. Do you find joy in every day? How will you feel if your child seems to prefer one parent over another, or even a grandparent? What are the values you want to instill in your child? Practice a daily ritual of reflection.

MANAGE EXPECTATIONS. Understand basic developmental milestones, knowing that children reach them at a variety of times. Write down how you hope to see your child at five years old, at 10, at 15, 25, and 30. Keep these to yourself. As your child reaches those milestones, reread your expectations. You will be delighted at your child's independence and choices.

FIND COMMON GROUND WITH YOUR PARTNER. Take some time for you and your partner to reflect on each of your childhoods. Ask yourselves "Was I given choices? Were my parents authoritarian or liberal? What expectations were there for grades, work, play? Was I allowed to express my thoughts, feelings?" Compare your notes with your partner's. Do you want to raise your child the same way either of you were raised?

EMBRACE FLEXIBILITY. You will be rearranging your space every few months to accommodate your developing child. You will have to reflect on how things are going for you and your family.

BE AN ACTIVE OBSERVER. Observation is a key component of Montessori. You can use a notebook, videos—whatever is readily available. Record the date, time, and place and write an objective blurb about what your child did and what happened before and right after.

INSTILL WONDER, JOY, AND CURIOSITY. Start a daily journal of things to be grateful for, people you want to connect with, goals for the day, week, year, and life. Rekindle the appreciation and wonder of life that you want your child to feel.

FOLLOW YOUR CHILD'S LEAD. Be prepared and learn to let them take the lead on their interests. I learned to understand the rules of soccer and baseball and managed teams for 10 years. I never took the field myself, but I engaged in my son's love of sports.

ASK THEM QUESTIONS. This develops memory, inventiveness, creativity, and curiosity in your child. By 24 months, you can start asking how, what, where, and why questions.

FAMILY DYNAMICS

As I mentioned previously, a sense of security is critical to a child's development. Ultimately, the more parents and caregivers can agree about child-rearing philosophies, the greater stability the child will have. It is important to partner with all of the adults who will be interacting with your child. This could mean helping grandparents and babysitters understand your ideas and requests so that your child has consistent interactions with all of the adults in their life.

With your partner or spouse, this means understanding each other's upbringing and views on parenting. People tend to model their parenting styles on how they were raised, but it's likely you and your partner were not raised in exactly the same way. So, ask each other: What about your childhood did you find healthy? What do you wish your parents had done differently?

You may also want to ask:

- How do you feel about the sounds of a baby crying?

- How do you feel about co-sleeping with an infant?

- What are your feelings on children following directions?

- How comfortable are you with children taking risks?

- Who, including specific family members and friends, are you comfortable around?

- What religion, if any, do you want to raise them in?

Once you've answered these questions, decide which is flexible and which is nonnegotiable. You will discover differences; that's natural. But it's better to find them out early on, so you can work through them together.

Should you be a single parent, ask yourself these questions so you know your ideals. Then, when you bring other adults into your child's life, you can express your preferences.

If this is not your first child, you'll want to prepare siblings for the new arrival. Use the baby's name or say "baby" when referring to the addition to the family. Leave out "new." Typically, in the eyes of a child, old things are no longer loved or kept. Empower an older child to help you prepare for the baby by choosing toys, colors, clothes, and the like.

Once the baby arrives, allow the older sibling or siblings to take ownership of orienting the baby to the family. Have them tell stories to the baby about family vacations, dinners, the dog, Grandpa. Give your older child or children the chance to feel that they are important in your life.

THE DOS AND DON'TS OF MANAGING YOUR CHILD'S BEHAVIOR

Montessori believed that children acquire self-discipline by absorbing the moral customs and attitudes around them. Learning to control their small and large muscles are also part self-discipline.

Understanding what is developmentally appropriate for the age of your child is fundamental. From birth to about 18 months, a child is not capable of understanding the mores and rules of their new world. It is not possible to spoil them. They need a secure, safe, predictable environment to develop in.

From about 18 months on, toddlers begin to control their body movements. They need to be presented with activities that engage their large and small muscles to work toward developing concentration and mastery of movements.

Children learn consequences of their actions from the beginning. They can understand the verbalization of consequences "When you scream, it hurts my ears." "The cat is not happy when you pull her tail."

Temperament is another important factor. Are they flexible (easy), feisty (difficult), or fearful (slow to warm)? Remember to look at a situation through the child's point of view.

Montessori Dos and Don'ts

▶ **Do** ask yourself if the behavior is developmentally appropriate. If so, try to change your expectations and mindset.
Don't set unrealistic expectations for your child's developmental stage.

▶ **Do** use the techniques of giving choices, redirection, and explaining consequences.
Don't use time-outs, charts, or rewards, and don't take away anything to control the child. Never hit a child.

▶ **Do** ask yourself if the activity/behavior is safe; if not, change the environment, material, or schedule.
Don't forget to review the environment, schedules, and materials daily.

▶ **Do** model respect for your child, other people, materials, and how you move around your house. Use positive, caring, peaceful tones and words.
Don't treat people, items, or the way you move about in your life with disrespect. Don't use negative, sarcastic, or demeaning language. Don't carry grudges.

▶ **Do** acknowledge your own mistakes and explain how you learned from them.
Don't make your child feel guilty for not doing something that is beyond their ability.

▶ **Do** speak positively, acknowledging their emotions. Problem solve by having your child come up with "instead of" options for next time.
Don't indulge in long verbal criticisms.

▶ **Do** show patience. Always remember the long-term goal is having your child learn the appropriate behavior.
Don't react just for the moment. Never take it personally.

Preparing the Environment (That's Your House!)

The Montessori environment is comprised of three components: the actual layout and furniture, the materials and activities provided, and the adult guide/parent/teacher who is responsible for observing the child. Having said that, the size of your living quarters or of your wallet does not matter. Montessori can be done in any amount of space and on any budget. It is the attitude and the general understanding of the principles that matter.

You may start with one or a few areas of your home and then, as your child grows, bring Montessori into more aspects of your life and space.

Here are some general rules for setting up an environment:

1. **Safety.** Look at your home through the eyes of your child. Are there any inviting things they can go after that could cause a disaster? You want your child to feel secure. Having to say "That is not safe" discourages confidence and independence. (See guidelines on page 31.)

2. **Keep things simple.** Montessori is all about keeping things simple and practical. For toddlers and older children, have low shelves with two or three items displayed to choose from.

3. **Enrich their senses.** Keep in mind your child's sensory development at all ages. You want them to touch all sorts of textures; taste all kinds of foods; smell indoor and outdoor scents; hear city and country sounds, music, and nature; and see the beauty in the world, both big and small.

4. **Freedom for exploration and movement.** Movement lets the brain, muscles, and senses work together, allowing children to build confidence and independence. Create safe areas, however small, for them to explore. Keeping toddlers in seats or walkers for long periods of time limits their ability to move about. Let your child walk whenever possible.

5. **Make things accessible.** Place various objects and tasks within your child's reach—such as a low hook for a toddler's coat or a mobile for an infant—and encourage them to use them.

6. **Keep things clean.** Cleanliness shows respect for the child and all who live in the space. It shows that you want your child to see and appreciate the world around them.

7. **Declutter.** For the well-being of your child (and for your own well-being), make sure to maintain a sense of order. The less time you spend looking for objects or toys, the more you engage with your child.

8. **Let children own their space.** We all take pride in projects we "own," such as baking a cake or mowing the lawn. Children do, too. Give them age-appropriate jobs in their spaces, such as misting the plants or wiping off the table after lunch. Watch them shine as they develop mastery, confidence, and pride.

9. **Incorporate the natural world.** Montessori believed in the importance of nature. Studies since then have backed her up: Being in nature improves concentration, relieves stress, and more. Bring nature inside with safe houseplants and materials made from natural materials, such as wood instead of plastic.

Safety First

Safety is the number one priority for all children at all times at all ages. A prepared environment is a safe environment. Let's go over a few general safety guidelines:

Keep children in your sightline. Whether outside or indoors, children younger than three should be within your sight at all times. Even infants have the capacity to roll over and hurt themselves.

It's back to sleep. Infants should sleep in their own bassinet, on their back, with no bumpers, with no blankets (a sleep sack is best), with no stuffed toys, and with no mobiles, and within an arm's reach of you.

Get down to your child's eye level. Think like an exploring child. Do you see small objects on the floor they may choke on? Are there cords your child could pull on? Make sure strings, ribbons, cords, and ropes on pull toys are not longer than six inches.

Beware of small objects. If an object fits inside a toilet paper tube, a child should not be alone with it until they are older than three years. Also keep an eye on small parts that could come off of toys and stuffed animals.

Keep furniture safe. At about two years old, some children can open the bottom drawers of a dresser and climb up. Once they're mobile, children can pinch their fingers in a doorjamb. Keep a step ahead of your child's development and install safety devices when needed.

Watch what they eat. The CDC has a list of items that children younger than two should not be given to eat because they are choking hazards. Be mindful of food allergies and sensitivities.

Be careful outdoors. Be aware of bees, wasps, ants, plants, and even your neighbors' not-nice dogs. Don't forget the sunblock and remember that little fingers get frostbitten faster than ours.

Watch the water play. Children love to play in water but be mindful. A child can drown in three inches of water.

Always buckle up. Always buckle up children in car seats. Read the manufacturer's directions and have your careseats properly installed. Many local police, emergency medical services, or fire departments will help you. Put on those bike helmets.

Sign up for recall email lists. Manufacturers will send you emails whenever children's clothing, equipment, or toys are recalled for safety reasons. Sign up for email notifications.

Take safety classes. There are free online and in-person classes for new parents and caregivers in cardiopulmonary resuscitation, first aid, sudden infant death syndrome, shaken baby syndrome, and poison control. Check with your local health department.

Selecting Materials and Activities

Now that you have chosen your Montessori space and laid out the area, it's time to select and prepare the materials and activities. Whatever you select the goal is to excite your child, give them a sense of joy and wonder, and arouse their curiosity. Also consider items that will slightly challenge them yet maintain their desire to stick with the activity until they master it. Consider planning activities such as telling stories and singing songs. You will see some of these activities in the chapters ahead.

Montessori materials and activities are designed to address and engage the physical, social, emotional, cognitive, and moral development of the child. For example, if your child needs to improve their balance, place a strip of tape on the floor and have them try to walk along it without stepping off. Once they master that have them walk along the tape while carrying something light in one hand, and then again with progressively heavier objects. In this activity the child is being challenged, having fun, and improving their strength, balance, and body control.

Typically, young children will return to an activity countless times until it is mastered, and then more times for the pleasure of accomplishment. The repetition of physically mastered tasks and met goals boosts a sense of self-confidence, independence, and self-discipline.

There are thousands of Montessori activities, especially for children from birth to age three, that allow them to explore, name, categorize, and refine their senses. Many Montessori materials can be found on the Internet or elsewhere (see Resources, page 134, for some ideas.) Once you understand the concepts, you'll be able to create additional activities yourself.

Remember, even if you don't have the prepared space or many materials, you can apply Montessori by talking and reading to your child daily. This is a key to developing language, vocabulary, grammar, and syntax. Read to your infant at least daily, often a few times a day (see Resources, page 134, for suggestions). Be mindful of the books you bring into your home. Do they show the diversity of the world? Your child should see pictures that are familiar to them and also pictures that expose them to other customs and experiences of others.

Part 2 of this book will provide you with lots of materials and activities specific to the various stages of your child's development. Many of the materials may already be found in your home or can be made.

BEST PRACTICES

The golden rule when it comes to engaging in an activity with your child is to make sure they enjoy doing it with you. What's more, when they master it ensure that they enjoy doing it by themselves.

Here are a few tips to keep in mind when you implement the activities in part 2.

- From your observations, determine if your child is developmentally ready for the activity. If not, then save it until they will be able to succeed.

- Before presenting new material, be sure your child has the energy and is not too hungry or tired to be excited about the material.

- Be dramatic when you present an activity. Show your child with your facial expressions and vocal intonations just how excited you are.

- Children are great mimics, so let them imitate you. If you shake the maraca, they will shake the maraca. If you stack blocks, they will stack blocks. If you wipe the table, they will wipe the table.

- Start slow. When presenting an activity slowly demonstrate, from start to finish. Ask your child if they would like a turn when you are finished. When they are finished, show them where the materials should be stored. If your child is not interested or the activity appears too difficult, put it away for another day.

- Keep an eye on what your child has mastered and think of new challenges. Activities that a child will be able to do will change every few months.

THE THREE-POINT LESSON

This is the classic way Maria Montessori presented a new word to children. When trying to develop a child's vocabulary and memory, Montessori recommends presenting material in what is known as the three-point lesson. This activity can be done with colors, numbers, shapes, animals, or any objects in the home. The goal is to help the child learn the name of an object, identify it, and recall its name. Children love to play this and are quite proud of themselves as they acquire more and more vocabulary.

1. First, tell the child the name of something, such as a toy or image, while you point to it or hold it.
   Example: "**This is** an elephant; can you say 'elephant'?"

2. Next, ask the child to show or point to the object.
   "Can you **show me** (or point to) the elephant?"
   If the child doesn't do it, repeat the first step. If the child points, move to the third step.

3. Point to the object and ask the child to name it.
   "**What is** this?"

Remember to keep it short and simple, presenting one object/concept/word at a time: "this is," "show me" (or point to), and "what is."
   The three-point lesson is also used to define concepts: "This is a small cat."/"This is a big cat."

Montessori and Technology

Montessori believed children learn best through manipulation, movement, and exploring objects. She also believed in following the child as they follow their interests to create meaningful learning. Even though children can be enchanted by screen activity, that practical life activity doesn't lend itself to be incorporated into the Montessori way.

The American Academy of Pediatrics recommends that "children that are under the age of two years old should not have any screen time. At these younger stages, your child's eyesight has not developed enough for tracking motion or depth perception. Although these abilities will develop over the first year of life, exposure to screen time during this period is deemed unsafe."

For these reasons, many Montessori licensing agencies forbid schools to have any screen time for children younger than two, and then limit screens to 30 minutes a day for those aged two to six.

While children may not use screens, technology has made its way into Montessori homes and classrooms in other ways. For example, music is played over various devices, apps record children's activities, and FaceTime is used for older children to stay connected with family.

Today's reality is that parents are busy, and tablets and TVs can keep a child interested in a pinch. As long as your two-year-old does not get a steady diet of screen time and is buoyed by plenty of active time, they will thrive.

Part 2

Montessori in Action

In part 2, we review of your child's first three years and the development that will take place physically, socially, emotionally, and morally during each stage. I suggest some ways to prepare to bring Montessori into your child's daily life for each year. I also have descriptions of movement, sensory, and language activities, as well as sidebars on toileting, behavior management, safety, and more. In the last chapter, you'll learn about options for your preschool child's next steps.

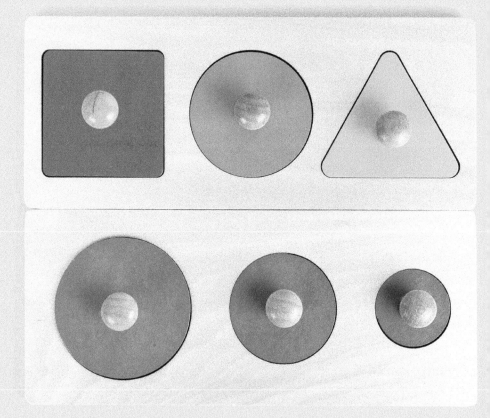

Welcome Home: The First Year

Your little infant will grow so much and so fast in their first year.
In this chapter, I will show you ways to tweak your environment,
point out development milestones that—before you blink—your child
will be achieving, and then provide you with a collection of activities for your child's sensory, motor, and communications delight.

A Rich, Sensory Environment

Congratulations on your newborn (or soon-to-be newborn) child! The
first year as parents is an incredibly rewarding time, replete with joy
and discovery. It will be astonishing to see your child grow so quickly
right before your eyes.

Montessori referred to this earliest stage of life as the period of
the unconscious mind (see page 7). During this critical moment of
development, a child takes in everything in their environment. They
acquire all their information through their senses: sight, sound,
smell, taste, and touch. This information gives them knowledge
about the world around them and ignites their imagination. Your
infant is also in a sensitive period for brain development. At its

peak, your infant's brain will make an astounding 2 million synapses a second, creating the many neural connections necessary for their rapid growth. The more sensory input a child receives at this age, the more synapses their brain makes. These cannot be made up later in life.

It's very important that the adults provide an environment rich in sensory experiences. In generations past, it was commonly thought that parents should merely care for their child—feed them, bathe them, nap them. Montessori showed that much more is necessary for them to achieve their fullest potential—determined not only by their *ability* (what they are born with) but also by *opportunity* (what is made available to them in their environment). She considered an infant's environment, as well as the didactic materials and pedagogy of the adults interacting with them. We will explore all of this—and more—in the pages to follow.

Keep in Mind

As you read this chapter and implement Montessori's teachings into your child's life during their first year, here are a few things to remember.

You know your child better than anyone else. Montessori trained her guides to partner with parents when caring for and educating children with this in mind. When in doubt, go with your gut.

Your child will always love you best. Even if it feels like they don't love you, when you have to have necessary boundaries and limits.

Make your infant feel secure, to feel comfortable exploring their world. Hold them and speak to them lovingly. You want to help them feel secure in their decision to crawl (and eventually walk) away, knowing they'll always have you to return to.

Health and wellness helps them grow in many ways. As a doctor, Montessori's initial concern was for the health of the children. Healthy food, regular checkups, immunizations, and sleep are critical.

Put your baby down, when possible. Let them learn to maneuver their bodies on their own. Montessori's freedom of movement starts when you bring them home.

Give infants safe objects to grasp and shake. Let their small muscles get a workout as they discover all that their fingers are able to do.

Indulge their senses. Provide infants with an array of sensory experiences. Observe them when they taste new foods and smell different scents.

Your Child's Development

Over the course of their first year, babies typically learn to manage their limbs. They learn to control their fingers, crawl, sit up, stand, and walk. They begin to understand and respond to spoken language, using gestures and even a few words (sometimes, in two languages) to communicate. They learn to indicate when they are hungry and full, and even start to feed themselves. Socially and emotionally, babies are quickly becoming individuals with their own likes and dislikes.

It's important to remember that each child develops at their own pace. This is why the Montessori method respects each child at whatever level of functioning they've reached and responds in kind to help them take the next step.

PHYSICALLY. Infants are totally dependent on adults. They are born with dozens of reflexes, and they usually double their birth weight in four months. They grow hair, get teeth, roll over, crawl, sit up, stand up, cruise, and, eventually, start to toddle and walk.

EMOTIONALLY. Our sense of self-worth starts to develop in infancy. When babies cry, they are reaching out to the world to let it be known that they are hungry, tired, uncomfortable, or bored. When the cry is answered, they know that they are being attended to—that they have "worth." This helps them build self-confidence.

SOCIALLY. Infants see and hear the interactions of those around them. They may not understand your words, but they are aware of the tones and the volume of the voices. They can see and feel different facial expressions, such as smiles and frowns. You smile, they smile; you babble, they babble. This is early socialization.

COGNITIVELY. Our capacity to learn declines as we age: We learn more in infancy than in any other stage of life. Your infant is absorbing language and learning to quantify things in the world around them. So, for example, by the end of their first year, they will likely be able to communicate your name verbally and indicate that they prefer a pile of 20 Cheerios over just one.

MORALLY. Children learn the mores of the society, and the household, into which they are born. This includes both language and customs—what is said and not said, done and not done, expressed and not expressed, believed and not believed. Even young infants will behave differently in different environments or with different people. They seem to know that grandparents will indulge them.

The Prepared Environment

It's an exciting time in your life, and there are many things to do to prepare for the arrival of your newborn. In this section, we'll touch on your baby's nursery from the Montessori perspective.

As we discussed in part 1, a Montessori environment is orderly, safe, and peaceful; filled with materials and space where a child can develop. A Montessori nursery is designed through the eyes of the infant, not the adults. The more you internalize the Montessori core concepts (see page 7), the easier it will be to incorporate Montessori's ideas into your own home. Whether you have an entire room in a house to devote to the Montessori environment or just one area of another room, the space you designate for your new child should be a bastion of orderly peace and beauty.

THE SLEEPING AREA

Sleep is vital to the growth and health of children (and the well-being of parents). Newborns typically sleep close to their mother as they may need to be nursed in the middle of the night. The Montessori way prefers the use of a bassinet. There should be only a fitted sheet in the bassinet—no bumpers, pillows, or stuffed animals.

Infants should always be put to sleep on their back until they are able to roll themselves over (typically, at about two months). Whenever you decide to move your child to a crib, be sure to adhere to the most current safety guidelines (see the Consumer Product Safety Commission website: cpsc.org). Antiques or heirloom cribs may be nice, but they may not be safe. The mattress should be new and firm. As with the bassinet, there should be no toys, stuffed animals, or mobiles in the crib. Your child should associate the crib with sleeping, not playing.

Remember, your little one is taking everything in and absorbing their world. Make sure your newborn's nursery is visually calm and non-stimulating. Soothing nature sounds are associated with rest and peace. You can play (or make) recordings of the ocean's waves or a soft rain.

The Floor Bed Versus the Crib

Montessori believed that children could self-regulate—that if they're tired, they could go to sleep of their own volition. To promote sleep she provided low, child-size beds, about six inches off the floor, that babies could safely get into and out of by themselves. Today, many Montessori schools have floor beds for napping.

Some parents set up floor beds in their own homes, as well—starting as early as infancy—either in the parents' room or the child's bedroom. Of course, every family is different, and you will need to evaluate whether a floor bed would work for yours. If you plan on using one, the entire space needs to be prepared beforehand to keep the child safe as if they could wake up and begin to crawl. Because some day they will. Eliminate small items and cords they can pull. Cover all electrical outlets. With floor beds, you need to be especially cognizant of any area your child could wedge themselves into, or any door through which they could leave the room.

By contrast, a crib allows parents to keep track of exactly where the child is while resting and at night. Additionally, some children like the security of a crib. It may be best to start your child off in a crib and switch over to a floor bed as they get a bit older and request more independence. Because of this and other safety concerns, many parents will wait until the child is closer to three years old to set up a floor bed.

THE PLAY SPACE

Montessori believed that a child's "work"—what one is meant to do—is play. Children go to "work" to learn about their world—how to understand it, navigate it physically, connect with the people in it, and master tasks associated with it. The play space should make this work possible. Your goal is to transform your child's environment into a space where your child can explore what they see and where (safe) things are within their reach.

You may set aside a whole room or section off part of a room. Be sure to look at it from your child's perspective. Keep everything organized: textured, washable, easy-to-grip objects in one basket, soft cloth objects in another, board books up right on a shelf.

Before your child is mobile, you're responsible for bringing materials (toys) to them and introducing the object by engaging with it yourself. If it's a rattle, for example, you'll want to shake it until their eyes travel to the sound. Then, shake it again. Finally, you'd want to place it in their hand and shake it together.

As mentioned before, safety is paramount, so be sure to conduct a safety check of the play space (see page 31) and make sure your child can't crawl or toddle out of the area. Keep adult objects out of sight and reach.

Let's Explore!

As you'll recall from chapter 1, a child's first year falls firmly in Montessori's sensitive period for sensory learning. In your own home, you can create an environment that will help your child refine their senses and glean information about the world around them. Look around your home. What is your child seeing? Is it pleasing to the eye? Soothing? Uncluttered? Orderly? If things aren't, invest in some baskets or boxes to reflect a sense of organization and respect for materials.

Keep in mind, too, that the sense of touch involves not only what the child touches with their fingers, but also what touches them. Some infants experience irritation or allergic reactions when they come in contact with certain fabrics, floor coverings, and carpets.

Massages are another wonderful option for babies. They stimulate the nerve endings in the skin, thereby sending more information about the sense of touch to the brain, aiding in their development. Work massage time into your daily routine.

As your child moves through their first year, consciously expose them to their world. Follow their eyes and say out loud what they are seeing, smelling, or hearing. For example, you could go for a walk and say, "Do you see this flower? It is red. Would you like to smell it?"

Montessori Says:

Montessori spoke often about the importance of children interacting with the world around them. "The hand is the instrument of intelligence," she said in her 1946 London Lectures. "The child needs to manipulate objects and to gain experience by touching and handling."

ACTIVITY #1
Let's Touch Different Textures!

Description: Children's tactile senses pick up information from their whole body, not just their fingers. This activity allows the infant to experience various textures while socializing with others or observing a mobile.

Materials: A yard of fabric, a safe floor space

PEDAGOGY:

1. Place your child on their back in a diaper (room temperature permitting) on an approximately 3-by-3-foot square of fabric, such as a pillowcase or blanket.
2. Engage your child by smiling, talking, singing, babbling, having fun, and observing them touching and feeling the surface texture. You can say descriptive words (soft, fuzzy, smooth), even though your child will not yet understand the meaning.
3. Infants up to about three months old should enjoy this activity for about five to seven minutes.

Montessori Extension: Expose your child to different textures. Terry cloth towels, linen tablecloths, satin pillowcases, wool blankets, yoga mats, are just a few items you may have in your house.

ACTIVITY #2
Let's Taste and Smell What We're Eating!

Description: From infancy on, parents should tease their baby's senses of taste and smell. Once your child starts eating food in addition to breast milk or formula (typically at about six to 12 months) watch their reaction to the taste. Do they make a face at peas? Open wide for applesauce? Observe their awareness of differences in taste and smell. Letting them choose—within reason—the food they prefer helps them develop independence and self-regulation.

Materials: A handful of Cheerios

PEDAGOGY:

1. Wash your hands.
2. Sit across from your child in their feeding spot at eye level.
3. Break a few Cheerios in half and place them within arm's reach of the child on their tray.
4. Describe the Cheerios. "This is a Cheerio. It is crunchy. It sticks to your fingers. Do you want to taste it? Can you put it into your mouth? Do you like it?"
5. Share the snack and tell your child, "I like to eat these Cheerios."
6. Be observant when your child gives you signs that they are full—this encourages self-regulation.
7. Always make sure they are sitting while eating.

Montessori Extension: Infants put everything in their mouths. Use this to your advantage to refine their sense of taste and smell. Try each new food for a week before introducing another. This allows time to see if your child has any reactions such as a rash, gas, or diarrhea.

ACTIVITY #3
Let's See What's in the Basket!

Description: Children love to touch and manipulate objects, and they love to move about. They also love to put things inside other things and dump them out. At around nine months fill a basket with small objects of different textures for the child to dump out. Do this over and over. They will see a one-to-one correspondence between objects and numbers, absorbing the concept of rote counting (that is, counting numbers sequentially) for later use in math activities.

Materials: A basket (preferably made of a natural material, like hemp) and five small blocks with the same characteristics (size, shape, color, texture), or other toys a nine-month-old can grip

PEDAGOGY:

1. Sit down on the floor facing your child.
2. Show them your basket.
3. Take out the blocks one by one, placing them on the floor in front of you. As you take them out, count "one, two, three, four, five," with each number corresponding to each subsequent block.
4. Talk about the blocks "They are blue. They feel smooth."
5. Put them back in the basket one by one, counting the same way as in the previous step.
6. Invite your child to play with you, and then repeat steps 3 and 4 with your child.
7. Return the basket to the shelf so that your child knows where to find it next time.

Montessori Extension: Change what you put in the basket—from different shapes to animal figurines. Use descriptive words. Maintain a sense of wonder for your child each time you play this game.

Let's Move!

Birth to age two and a half is the sensitive period for movement, which is critical for two aspects of a child's development: their coordination and freedom with limits (see page 9).

During their first year, children are learning how to operate and control their neck, arms, legs, hands, and tongue—all at the same time. Considering how fast they're growing, they need to recalculate this coordination frequently. Constrained children do not get to practice all of these movements; they must instead make up for it later.

How does freedom with limits pertain to your little one, who does not seem to be going anywhere? Provided that they can see and hear you, infants who are safely placed on the floor will delight in figuring out how to worm about to get to their desired destination. This allows for physical development, as well as emotional development. The child will feel a sense of accomplishment for their adventure and will gain the confidence necessary to continue exploring their world. Keep in mind, your infant will be crawling and then walking before you know it. That's why the "limits" aspect of freedom with limits is so key—you can't just let the little ones go wherever their curiosity takes them.

Montessori Says:

"Children acquire knowledge through experience in the environment," Montessori said in her 1946 London Lectures. And in order to experience this environment, she believed they must engage with it. Physically, this entails practicing coordination of movement.

ACTIVITY #1
Let's Explore the Floor!

Description: Tummy time is when an awake infant is placed on their stomach so they can build up the arm and neck muscles required for crawling. In this activity, you'll provide a safe place for your child to worm around and wiggle in, until they eventually learn to crawl. Your infant will need to have developed some muscle control in their neck to do this activity, which could happen at any point from one to two months old.

Materials: A sanitized rattle (or otherwise visually enticing grab toy)

PEDAGOGY:

1. Make sure the environment is clean, safe, and visually and auditorily appealing. Laying a blanket or cloth down is a good idea, as it defines the play area and will likely be familiar to your child at this point.

2. Put your baby on their tummy onto the floor.
3. Place the rattle an inch beyond the baby's reach.
4. Get down on your tummy and face the baby. Shake the rattle until they can clearly see and hear it.
5. Once they notice it, place the rattle back just out of the baby's reach. If necessary, hold their hand in yours and help them reach out to grab the toy.
6. Continue for about two minutes, but make sure to end it before the baby is tired of the activity.

Montessori Extension: Add new grab toys and gradually place them a tad farther away. Eventually, your baby will worm over to grab the toy, increasing their physical development, confidence, and sense of independence.

ACTIVITY #2
Let's Pull Ourselves Up!

Description: As your infant inches closer to their first birthday, their muscles will have strengthened and they'll probably want to pull themselves up. From a standing position, they'll be able to survey their world with a fresh perspective, while developing the balance they'll need to walk. Use this activity to help your child—typically at about 10 to 14 months—accomplish this task.

Materials: A soft ottoman or couch

PEDAGOGY:

1. Place your child in a safe environment in which they are comfortable crawling around.
2. Add in an ottoman or place them near the couch so they can use it to pull themselves up to a standing position.
3. Once your child masters pulling themselves up, place a desired grab toy just beyond where they are standing. Watch them figure out how to move closer in order to grab it.

4. After success with the ottoman, situate your infant next to more furniture they can safely pull up on (the rounded edge of a low coffee table, perhaps).

Montessori Extension: A mirror against the wall near where your child is learning to pull themselves up will bring added delight to their experience. Alternatively, you can add photos of nature or family members to the mirror for them to see when they reach the standing position.

ACTIVITY #3
Let's Splash!

Description: Every baby loves the feel of water. After all, it's what they were encased in for nine months. Let them splash about and discover the effects of their movements.

Materials: Towel, pool, diapers

PEDAGOGY:

1. Test the water temperature of the pool to make sure it's not too hot or too cold.
2. Carry your baby step by step into a pool slowly.
3. Holding your baby firmly, move their arm for them to create a splash in the water. Watch their facial reactions.
4. Talk to your infant through the whole adventure. "We are going to go into the pool now" "Do you feel the water?" "It is wet." "Do you like it?"
5. Take the baby out after a few minutes and wrap them in the dry towel.

Montessori Extension: You may find a pool in your area that offers swim lessons for young children. It is not only a sensory activity, it is also good for physical activity/exercise. If you don't have access to a pool, your bathtub works well.

Let's Express Ourselves!

Montessori believed a sensitive period for language acquisition started at birth. Babies make sounds and gestures to indicate their needs and wants—the most wonderful, of course, being their smile.

Montessori often referred to the unconscious mind to explain how a child absorbed a world full of language, which they could then use to define and distinguish between experiences and information acquired through their senses. So while we have to be patient and wait for them to start talking, we also must fill their lives with language. There are many ways to accomplish this. Talk or sing to your child often. Tell them what is happening, what you are going to do or have done.

As your infant progresses though their first year, they will learn that certain sounds mean certain things. They start off naming things and move on to one- or two-word sentences to get a concept across. By their first birthday, they typically know the names of people and pets in their world.

Not enough can be said about the importance of reading to your child from infancy on. Books offer a wealth of vocabulary words rarely uttered in our daily lives. Who has a train track, or a penguin, or an airplane in their home? Nobody.

Montessori Says:

We are all impatient to hear in the child's own words how they feel, what questions they have, and what they have learned about our world. Montessori told us we have to be patient. "All children pass through a period in which they can only pronounce syllables," she wrote in *The Absorbent Mind*. "Then they pronounce whole words, and finally, they use to perfection all the rules of syntax and grammar."

ACTIVITY #1
Let's Talk!

Description: All children are born with a desire to communicate and do so by crying out, gesturing, and babbling. Starting at just two months, infants will copy smiles and sounds from others. This activity sets the stage for the child to understand the art of conversation.

PEDAGOGY:

1. When you are changing your infant or just making faces with them, listen for their babble.
2. Look your baby in the eyes. When they stop babbling, start babbling, singing, or otherwise verbally communicating for a few seconds.
3. When you stop, listen for them to babble back. When they do, show delight in your facial expression.
4. Repeat this cycle back and forth.

Montessori Extension: Repeat different sounds when you babble and notice if your child comes close to imitating the sounds you make. This rudimentary back-and-forth introduces your child to the art of conversation. With practice, your child will begin to love to interact, copy some of the sounds you make, use mouth muscles, and start to associate sounds with people and objects.

ACTIVITY #2
Let's Read!

Description: All infants love to have the same books read to them over and over. It gives them a sense of order and security, while honing their memory skills, as they begin to understand what to expect as you turn each page.

Books for infants should have simple, realistic pictures, preferably one to a page, with variations on each page. This activity demonstrates the Montessori method for presenting new material to children. First, name/identify something. Then, see if the child can recognize it. Finally, see if they can recall the name of the object.

Materials: A board book

PEDAGOGY:

1. Ask your child, "Do you want to look at this book with me?"
2. Place them on your lap and snuggle up together.
3. Model how to hold the book and turn the pages.
4. Talk a bit about the book: "This is a book about cats. Let's look at all of the cats."
5. Point to a photo or picture in the book and identify it: "This is a cat."
6. Prompt them to point to the figure you just pointed to: "Where is the cat?"
7. Ask them: "What is this?" At about 15 months, they may be able to repeat the name back to you.

Montessori Extension: Start a small collection of board books for your child's play area. For infants, stand the books up so they can crawl to them. Books with textured pages give infants a chance to touch and feel the pages.

ACTIVITY #3
Let's Listen to Music!

Description: Auditory perception—the ability to distinguish sounds—is the basic building block needed to use Montessori's language materials, such as object boxes and the movable alphabet, for children around age three. By exposing infants to different tones, styles of music, and the like, they become more aware of the endless variety of sounds instruments and voices can make.

Materials: A computer or device to play music

PEDAGOGY:

1. Curate a selection of music to play for different times of the day.
2. If it is bedtime, for example, choose music your child will associate with going to sleep at night, like a quiet lullaby.
   If it is playtime, choose the music your child will associate with movement, like a lively dance song.
3. Remember to give vocabulary to the sounds. Use words to name and describe sounds: "Do you like this Mozart music?" "This country music makes me want to move my body."

Montessori Extension: Make sure the volume of any music is at an appropriate level, not too loud. Expose your child to a range of music—classical, folk, pop, show tunes, jazz, what have you. Listen to what you enjoy and they, too, will develop a love of music.

Before You Move On . . .

Congratulations! As your child's first birthday approaches, remember that this celebration is really for you. You have guided your child from an infant to a toddler. They can likely move about on their own, and communicate with words. They're turning into a social creature who is a delight to be around. You showed them how to respect themselves, their possessions, and their parents. You gave them the opportunity to move about, to gain self-esteem and confidence. Now that your infant is a toddler, your environment and the way you communicate will need to change.

Here are a few points to consider as you move on to the next year of your child's life:

- Toddlers can get into so many more places than infants. Get down to their eye level and look at the world through their eyes. What can they now reach, climb to, or get ahold of?

- Verbal communication blossoms in toddlers. Start to think about which books from your local library you can borrow to supplement your collection.

- Toddlers are starting to express their likes and dislikes of food, toys, and people. Be cognizant of these preferences. Remember to follow their lead.

- Keep in mind there will be a lot more to observe in your child this year. Look out for a burst of independence as they get closer to the 24-month mark.

From Infant to Toddler: The Second Year

As you celebrate your child's first birthday, you should also celebrate your one-year anniversary of parenthood. Congratulations! In this chapter, I will go over the developmental milestones you should expect in this coming year and how you can organize your environment to accommodate your child's growing needs. I will go over toileting and provide some activities to try out with your child. Enjoy this special year.

Exploring Their World

During your child's second year, it's important that you stick to Montessori's core concepts, while modifying your environment to adapt to a more mobile child. Materials and activities that activate your child's senses, facilitate greater independence, and enhance their verbal communication skills are important and necessary.

Typically, at about the one-year mark, children have realized they can pull themselves up and toddle about to get where they want to go. Their muscles are developing. With practice, they will improve their balance and sharpen control of their limbs. They will also begin to develop a keen interest in small objects, exhibit a greater attention to detail, and show an interest in what goes in and comes out of their bodies.

At this age, children are also learning to recognize and manage their emotions and their interactions with others. The second year lands firmly within Montessori's sensitive period for language. A toddler's brain is able to process speech more quickly than an infant's. Their ability to understand language is increasing. This year, your child will likely babble less, add new words to their vocabulary, and unconsciously store even more.

There are many more Montessori activities to expose your child to this year, some of which I'll highlight in this chapter. In this second year, your toddler will be moving about on their own and exploring their world. Growing up in a Montessori home will not only facilitate their development physically, socially, and cognitively, it will also further bolster their self-confidence and independence. Get ready for year two.

Keep in Mind

Here are a few things to keep in mind as you read this chapter and implement Montessori's teachings into your child's life during their second year.

Reexamine your environment through your toddler's eyes. Toddlers are constantly exploring and on the move. They're notorious for climbing up on furniture and then having it all fall down. Bolt things to the wall if necessary. Observe your child at all times.

Independence will start to surface. Dressing them will be much easier. Have clothes that are easy for you and your child to take off and on. Toddlers love to take off mittens, socks, and shoes. Avoid buttons, belts, and tie shoes.

Don't lock them out of the bathroom. Let them start to understand what a toilet is used for (see page 68).

Make meals a social event. Serve children bite-size portions of what you are eating and talk about the taste, texture, and temperature of the food. Discuss where the food came from and how was it prepared.

Expand your child's library. Include books with rhymes, rhythm, repetition, and realistic illustrations.

Give your child simple choices. "Would you like blueberries or apple slices for a snack?" "Do you want to put on your socks or do you want me to put them on for you?"

Practice counting skills. Make a habit of counting things off in fives: five stones, five jumps, five leaves. Children love this kind of orderly repetition.

Avoid saying "no," unless it's a serious situation. Instead, use positive words—"We use walking feet inside the house," "Nice touching the baby/dog"—or redirect your toddler. When adults say "no" too often, children start ignoring them.

Sleep schedules may change. At about 12 months, many children move to having only one nap a day. Observe your child for this transition.

Interests will ebb and flow. Sometimes, your child is just not interested in a given activity at a given time. In these cases, put it away and observe your child for an opportune time to present it again.

Your Child's Development

Your child has circled the sun once in their life. In their second year, you'll see them grow in new and wonderful ways.

PHYSICALLY. Your child will soon be walking, stooping, climbing stairs. They will begin to feed themselves, using a spoon and a cup, building block towers, drawing with crayons, and turning the pages of their favorite books. They may also start washing their hands and learning what goes in and comes out of their bodies. Generally, they sleep 12 to 14 hours a night and move to one nap a day.

EMOTIONALLY. Your child is developing greater self-control. For example, they can understand they are not supposed to grab the dog's treat, but they're still developing the control needed to refrain from doing so. They're amassing a bigger vocabulary, but they can't always express themselves as distinctly as they'd like. This can be quite frustrating, resulting in short tantrums. These will likely continue throughout the next year or so. These outbursts are a normal part of growing up. Have patience.

SOCIALLY. Your one-year-old will start to reach out socially, respond to their name, and begin to express their emotions. They will repeat sounds you make and start to use words. They'll show affection, attention, and preferences for people and things. At this age, they begin to play pretend, engage in parallel play and peekaboo.

COGNITIVELY. Your one-year-old is still busy exploring their world, touching, shaking, tasting, and throwing things, in order to discover what happens. Moreover, they are observing the consequences of their actions. This is a sensitive period for language acquisition (they'll learn about 50 words this year). They can typically understand much more of what you say to them. This year will be full of gestures and the beginnings of expressive language. Your child will also know your name and the names of other people (and pets if you have them) in your home. They can follow one-word directions.

MORALLY. Your child's unconscious mind is picking up the mores of your home and lifestyle. They are learning your language, growing accustomed to the smells of your cooking, beginning to eat your culture's food, and partaking in family rituals. Their moral development is absorbed through how you model conflicts, use your voice, and look at different kinds of people. They absorb your likes and dislikes.

The Prepared Environment

Now that your little one is walking (or toddling) about, you'll need to change their environment in accordance with these new abilities.

Indoors, new adventures await your mobile toddler. If your home has stairs, they'll likely gravitate toward them. Safety gates are a must. Only under parental supervision should your child practice going up and down stairs. Ramps are a good option for indoor walking. Use a flat board about three feet long; your child can also roll balls and toy cars down the ramp. Play tunnels are also great for active one-year-olds.

Your child's smaller muscles are being refined at this point, so it's a good idea to provide them with materials to exercise their fingers and hands, such as DUPLO sets and Playdough.

To accommodate your child's exploding language acquisition, fill your lives with poems, songs, finger puppet plays, and lots and lots of books. Fill containers in the play area with objects to spark your child's imagination and boost their vocabulary, such as small toy animals, pretend fruits, and blocks in various shapes and colors.

Now that your toddler can walk, they'll want to do it all day long. Visit a local park or playground. Go for a nature walk, and collect the wonderful treasures you find in a basket. Provide balls for children to roll, throw, and bounce. Have them run through the falling water from a sprinkler.

THE BEDROOM

In the second year, some parents move their toddler out of the crib to a floor bed. In Montessori schools, children use floor beds for naps, but there is always someone awake to monitor them. Since this isn't usually possible at home, you'll need to determine if a floor bed is practical for you (see page 45 for more on floor beds).

Children usually view rooms from the floor up to about three or four feet. You could paint the room one shade up to four feet and another shade above. Then place photos or paintings that you want your child to see in the lower half. Keep the room peaceful and be aware of all the sensory input your child can experience when they are trying to fall (and stay) asleep.

It's a good idea to install a low shelf within your child's reach, where they can place a favorite bedtime book, and a night-light or a noise machine that plays nature sounds. The shelf is also a good place for an unbreakable mirror and a comb to facilitate the child's morning routine.

If the bedroom has a closet or wardrobe, it's best to remove the doors and save them for when your child is older. Inside the closet, install two low hooks and a shelf within your child's reach. In the evening, hang up an outfit on each hook and place two sets of socks and underwear on the shelf. The next day, let your child choose which clothes they want to wear. Don't forget to include a child-size basket in the closet where your toddler can place their worn clothes.

Empowering children to make simple daily choices like this boosts their independence and self-esteem.

THE PLAY SPACE

Now that your child is a toddler, you'll want to make some changes to the play space that take into account their newfound mobility and development. In a Montessori classroom, children "work" in three main areas: the foyer (where they enter and leave the classroom), the food-prep area, and the play area.

At home, the foyer is where the family enters and leaves the home. A low bench here, for them to sit on and take off their shoes and a basket where they can store their shoes, is a great idea to foster independence. A few low hooks to store their jackets is also smart. If you don't have a foyer, place the bench, basket, or hooks as close to the front door as possible.

For the play area, child-size furniture is a must. You'll need chairs that your child can get in and out of on their own, a table about 18 inches off the floor is about the right size. A bookcase about 24 inches high and 36 inches wide is also ideal. The bookcase should be open.

The play area should be bright, inviting, and peaceful. On a low shelf, place two or three baskets. In each one, place five items to reinforce counting—five blocks, five toy cars, five toy bears, and the like. A second shelf might include a few board books and simple musical instruments, like a drum or a bell. Make sure that your child can see the cover of each book.

The furniture should be arranged so your child can move about freely within the limits of the space. This fosters independence, self-esteem, and confidence.

Food preparation at this age is mostly about orienting your child to where in the home food is stored, prepared, and eaten. They may help you sort groceries and count out items in a recipe. And just joining the family at meals models teaches them about sitting, conversing, and socializing.

THE BATHROOM

Undoubtedly, your child will grow curious about the bathroom. In all likelihood, they already love playing in the tub. Soon, they'll want to use the sink and investigate the toilet.

You should nurture their curiosity, but safety comes first. Start by placing medications in areas that children can't get to, and removing slippery bath mats.

In the tub, a mesh bag to hold water toys will help them drain well. In addition to cleaning themselves, children also love to clean the tub and the walls, so you may want to designate a few different-colored washcloths for this purpose.

The sink is usually the next adventure. Try placing a step stool beneath it. When your child stands on it, the sink is at armpit level. You should turn the water on and off, but your child can wash their own hands and face and brush their own teeth. Hang a towel on a low bar for them to reach.

Provide a damp cloth for them to wash their face. When it is time for brushing their teeth, the adult should squeeze a bit of toothpaste into a small unbreakable dish. Place it next to your child's toothbrush, along with a cup of water. If your mirror is up high, add one at the child's eye level so they can see what they're doing. In fact, why not have two brushes and let them choose which color they will use each time? Show your child how to dip the brush into the paste, brush it onto each tooth, and rinse their mouth. Toddlers are good at forming habits. Eventually they'll get better at it. They are forming good habits, and you are establishing an environment that allows freedom within limits.

Potty Training FAQs

From her extensive world travel, Montessori recognized that potty training varies by culture. In some, families potty train their child by the time they can walk; in others, potty training isn't considered until the child is about four years old and going off to school. Regardless of the cultural timing, most children grow up to be perfectly civilized children and adults.

Here are some frequently asked questions, answered:

I want to potty train my child. Where do I start?
To use the toilet, your child first has to understand what the toilet is for, so explain how it works and what it's for.

How do I show my child what a toilet is for?
Have them see it in use. Show them bowel movements from their diapers flushing away.

How do I help my child understand (and communicate about) their need to go?
It was critical to Montessori that children need to become aware of their bodies. You might start off with some basic questions: "Are you happy/mad?" "Are you hungry/full?" Eventually, these questions may lead to them being able to tell if they need to eliminate.

Once they can recognize when they need to go, how should they actually begin to use the toilet?
First, they'll need to master the skill of easily removing their clothing. Elastic waistbands are best. They should also practice getting on and off the toilet, first with their clothes on. When they can do these

things, and they understand what the toilet is for, you can tell them they're welcome to eliminate in the toilet when they feel the need. No flushing until they actually have put something in the toilet. After the child demonstrates success for a number of days, you may introduce them to cloth underwear instead of diapers. Expect accidents for months afterward; this is normal.

How long will it take for my child to be toilet trained?
All children eventually master it—usually by age five. Never make it an issue or get into a power struggle over it. Your child should maintain control over their body.

What if my child is okay during the day but still needs diapers at night?
Change to pull-ups or a different brand of diaper and refer to them as night pants or pajama pants. You do not want to confuse them by thinking it is acceptable to wear diapers some times and not wear them other times.

My child is mostly potty trained, but had an accident. What should I do?
Children will have accidents along the way. Do not give it too much attention; just be casual. Say something like, "I see you wet your pants. Do you want to take them off and put on dry ones yourself, or would you like my help?" Letting them decide how to solve the problem encourages problem-solving skills and resilience.

How are children toilet trained in Montessori classrooms?
As soon as children are able to walk, Montessori teachers bring them to the toilet to change them standing up. In time, the child is asked if they would like to sit on the toilet and eliminate into the toilet.

A child who has used the toilet gets to flush it and is then asked frequently during the day if they would like to sit on the toilet to eliminate, again. Flushing a toilet is a big "wow" for children.

Let's Explore!

The second year still falls firmly within the sensitive period for sensory learning. Continue to create an environment full of sensory experiences. Have your child observe you preparing meals. Let them touch and taste the ingredients and ask them to describe it all. Provide them with new words to communicate about their experience. Cooking is like magic to them. It is the beginning of wonder, the start of scientific inquiry.

While the activities in this section cultivate these experiences, they only scratch the surface. The possibilities to engage your child are endless. Perhaps it's an activity you're already passionate about, such as gardening, painting, or playing the piano. Introduce it to your child and allow them to take part in the fun.

Also, make sure you provide enough safe space, allowing them freedom to move about, explore their world, and choose activities. As your child gains physical dexterity, you can present them with opportunities to engage in more challenging activities that improve strength, endurance, balance, and coordination. Let them imitate your exercises or yoga routine. Encourage them to use all of their muscles, large and small.

Montessori Says:

The tiny child's absorbent mind finds all its nutriment in its surroundings. Here it has to locate itself, and build itself up from what it takes in. Especially at the beginning of life must we, therefore, make the environment as interesting and attractive as we can. The child, as we have seen, passes through successive phases of development and in each of these his surroundings have an important—though different—part to play. In none have they more importance than immediately after birth.
—*The Absorbent Mind*

ACTIVITY #1
Let's Make Bubbles!

Description: There is magic in bubbles. Children love to see them appear from the wand and float around. The bubbles call out to be touched. By popping the bubbles, children see the consequences of their actions. The more successful they are, the more bubbles they pop, bolstering their confidence to make further discoveries. Popping bubbles also helps them practice their hand-eye coordination.

Materials: A bottle of bubble solution, a bubble wand

PEDAGOGY:

1. Set yourself up in an outside area where your child can play.
2. With great enthusiasm, show the bottle of bubbles to your child: "Wow, what's inside this?"
3. Dip the wand into the bottle of bubble solution and blow some bubbles. Make sure your child sees them.
4. Show them what happens when you touch them. Act surprised when they disappear: "Where did it go?"
5. Encourage your child to pop some bubbles themselves.

Montessori Extension: Catch a bubble on the wand and have your child inspect it close-up, looking to see their reflection in the soapy water. This may help them practice their impulse control—that is, their restraint to look at, but not pop, the bubble. You might also have them blow on the bubbles themselves, which helps their mouth muscles develop.

ACTIVITY #2
Let's Use Playdough

Description: Playdough is a wonderful way to have your child use the small muscles of their fingers. Depending on what you mix in, Playdough also provides wonderful sensory touch experiences and can help children learn colors.

Materials: Store-bought or homemade Playdough (see Montessori Extension), airtight storage container, solid-color place mat

PEDAGOGY:

1. Put the place mat on the floor, a child-size table, or another solid surface. Place the container of Playdough on top.
2. Invite your child to take a look: "Look what I have today to work with."
3. Open the container, take out the Playdough, and knead it in your hands. Talk to your child, describing what you're doing: "This is Playdough. It's green. It feels soft. Would you like to touch it?"
4. Hand some Playdough to your child. Model how to squeeze it, shape it, and form it into a ball.
5. Explain that the Playdough should be kept on the place mat. When finished, demonstrate how it goes back into the container, with the lid on top. Then show your child where the Playdough container will be kept.

Montessori Extension: Once your child shows that they like Playdough and recognizes the meaning of "Do you want to play with the Playdough again?" you can show them how to make Playdough at home. This way, they can touch, see, smell, and even taste the ingredients.

HOMEMADE PLAYDOUGH RECIPE

Ingredients:

1 cup flour

¼ cup salt

¾ cup water

3 tablespoons lemon juice

1 tablespoon vegetable oil

5 small bowls

1 large bowl

1 storage container with lid

PEDAGOGY:

1. Premeasure all of the ingredients and place each in a separate small bowl.
2. Move the flour from the small bowl into the large bowl.
3. "This is flour. Would you like to smell it?"
4. Describe each of the other ingredients before adding them to the large bowl with the flour. For example, "This is salt, would you like to taste it?" "This is water. Would you like to touch it?"
5. Have your child help you knead the dough until it forms Playdough. Have fun playing.
6. When finished, put all of the Playdough into the airtight container, attach the lid, and show your child where it will be kept. It's best stored in the refrigerator.

ACTIVITY #3
Let's Play in the Sand!

Description: Once we reach adulthood, we tend to get much more information through our eyes and ears than through our sense of touch. Not so for toddlers. Few things have as interesting a texture as sand. Its granular nature, and its capacity to transform when water is added, prompts many new ideas and discoveries for children.

Materials: A 5-pound bag of sand, a plastic tub, floor covering, pitcher of water, three small containers, child-size hand shovel and rake

PEDAGOGY:

1. Put down the floor covering inside an area designated for this activity.
2. Put the sand in the tub and place it on the covering.
3. Invite your child to come and see what's in the tub.
4. Place your hand in the sand and describe it to them: "This is sand. It's dry. It feels rough."
5. Encourage your child to place their hands in the sand along with yours. Acknowledge the way the sand interacts with your hands: "The sand sticks to our hands."
6. Using the child-size hand shovel, scoop up the sand into the three smaller containers with your child. Remind them that the sand should stay in the container.
7. When you're finished, wash your hands together.

Montessori Extension: The next time you introduce this activity, add some water to change the sand's consistency and make it clump. Introduce other tools, such as spoons and child-size rakes. If you go to the beach, have your child touch the sand and fill the containers just like they did at home.

Let Me Do It Myself!

At this stage, children are still toying with the concept of independence. They're trying it out. So, you'll need to give them simple choices for which either option is correct. By properly preparing their environment, you allow your child to make a choice but not to make an error.

You can begin to implement Montessori's concept of "practical life" from a young age. For example, you can let a toddler hold on to their diaper and give it to you when you ask for it.

The child's ongoing quest for independence pulls in every aspect of development. Physically, they need to be able to move their body in all kinds of ways. Socially and emotionally, they need to identify and learn to express themselves. Cognitively, they need the freedom to think independently. To think for oneself and have the freedom to express those thoughts was a luxury in Montessori's world. Yet she recognized it as an integral part of the whole child.

Montessori Says:

The Montessori approach allows the child to be confident enough to try new things and realize when they might need help. This approach encourages them not to ask the adult to help them accomplish the task, but rather to help them learn how to do it themselves. "When the child is given a little leeway, he will at once shout out, 'I want to do it!'" Montessori wrote in *The Secret of Childhood*. "But in our schools, which have an environment adapted to children's needs, they say 'Help me to do it alone.'"

ACTIVITY #1
Let's Clean Our Face!

Description: From the moment your child turns one, they will put their fingers on the washcloth as you wash their face. They are curious: *Why is this wet, rough cloth on my face?* With this activity, you'll help your child answer that question and empower them to wash their face themselves, resulting in a sense of independence and accomplishment.

Materials: A damp washcloth

PEDAGOGY:

1. After your child is finished eating, introduce the concept of washing their face: "I am going to wash your face with the wet cloth. Would you like to help me?"
2. Show them the cloth and have them feel its texture and wetness in their hands. Point out that it is wet.
3. Together, use the cloth to wipe around your child's mouth. "Let's use the cloth to wash the food off of your face."
4. Let them wipe their face on their own.
5. If they've missed a spot, direct them to remove any remaining traces of food: "Let's get the rest of the food off together."
6. Show your child where the used cloth goes and tell them that they can wipe off themselves next time: "After meals, we always wash our face. You can wash your face again next time."

Montessori Extension: Have your child eat near or in front of a mirror so that they can see their face before and after a meal. They'll be able to see the consequences of using the washcloth.

ACTIVITY #2
Let's Brush Our Teeth!

Description: By age one, no matter how many teeth they have, it is good to have your child get into the routine of caring for their teeth daily. So, at the same time every day, such as just before sleeping, start the ritual.

Materials: A baby's first toothbrush (soft brush, small head, large handle), a mirror, a tiny bit of fluoride toothpaste in a saucer, small paper cup half filled with water

PEDAGOGY:

1. At the same time each day, say to your child, "Time to clean our teeth. Let's go to the bathroom and get out your toothbrush."
2. Have your child hold their toothbrush, put it under the running water, and dip it into a dish with a small amount (the size of a rice grain) of fluoride toothpaste.
3. Let your child look in the mirror and move the brush around inside their mouth for about 20 seconds while you sing the ABC song.
4. Then ask to see your child's teeth: "Let me see your clean teeth."
5. Have them rinse with a cup of water and then throw away the cup.

Montessori Extension: If they say okay to your doing the brushing, you can model/guide them how to move the brush.

ACTIVITY #3
Let's Put Away Our Toys!

Description: Children love order. If everything a child plays with has its own place, putting toys away is like solving a big puzzle. Eventually, your child will learn that before beginning a new activity, they should first put away the materials from the previous activity.

Materials: Your child's basket of blocks, or similar toys

PEDAGOGY:

1. Give your child a heads-up that it will soon be time to put away their toys so they can emotionally prepare to stop what they're doing and transition into the next activity.
2. Tell them: "I am looking for the red blocks. Let me see if I can find them." Then pick up the red blocks and put them in the basket. Repeat this step for the other toys in the basket.
3. See if your child brings you the desired object. If so, thank them and put it in the basket. If there are any toys left, ask: "What do we still have to put back in the basket?"
4. Thank your child for helping to collect any blocks they put in the basket.
5. When all of the toys are in the basket, announce: "All the blocks are in the basket. We can put the basket away now and take out the Playdough."

Montessori Extension: We all have to ask for help sometimes, and modeling this behavior is instructive for a child. It takes confidence to be willing to ask for help.

ACTIVITY #4
Let's Make a Snack!

Description: Children love to imitate their parents, especially when it comes to preparing food. The task gives them a huge confidence boost and a feeling of independence. This activity is best for children about 18 to 24 months old, who are orientated to where you store, prepare, and eat food in your home, and can carry a place mat, napkin, and bowl. Try doing this in the morning so they can carry this good feeling with them throughout the day.

Materials: Child-size table and chair, place mat, napkin, small bowl with two or three crackers, damp sponge in a sponge holder, bin for used dishes

PEDAGOGY:

1. Make sure all of the materials are on a nearby low shelf.
2. Wash your hands together and then demonstrate how to take out the place mat and put it on the table. Next, show your child where to place the napkin and the bowl of crackers.
3. Enjoy the snack with your child.
4. When finished, show your child where to place the napkin (in the trash) and where the dirty bowl goes (in the bin).
5. With the damp sponge, demonstrate how to wipe down the place mat. Then, show your child that the sponge goes back on the sponge holder and the place mat goes back on the shelf.
6. Finally, inform your child that starting tomorrow, there will be a snack for them to serve themselves whenever they feel hungry.
7. Wash your hands together, explaining: "We always wash our hands when we finish eating."

Montessori Extension: Once your child masters snack time, you can try leaving out cereal (as long as they have mastered pouring, see chapter 5). Think of everything your child would need, and put the materials on their low shelf, left to right in the order they're used.

ACTIVITY #5
Let's Help with Laundry!

Description: Starting at around 18 months, toddlers love to help around the house. Sorting clothes satisfies their tendency for order and helps them learn how to classify and put like things together. Their sense of independence and self-esteem comes from seeing what the adults are doing and feeling like they are contributing to the completion of the task.

Materials: An assortment of freshly clean laundry, preferably clothes that fall into a few categories, a clean sheet, baskets for each category of clothing

PEDAGOGY:

1. Place the sheet on the floor and the laundry on the sheet. Then, explore with your child: "These are your clean clothes from the washer and dryer. Let's smell them. How do they smell? Clean?"
2. Verbally assign each basket to a category: "All socks go in this basket; all shorts go in this basket. Let's sort them out and put them in their basket so that you can wear them this week."
3. Once they've completed the task, acknowledge their performance: "I see you sorted out all of your clothes. Do you want to show me where they go in your closet?"
4. If they're interested, have them help carry the baskets to their closet.

Montessori Extension: After everything is sorted, see if your child is interested in matching their socks, provided each set is unique. You might also help them pick out underwear and fold it, if they're so inclined.

ACTIVITY #6
Let's Garden!

Description: Being around nature is a wondrous experience for children. If you are fortunate enough to have a garden, let your child (of about 18 months) help out. Potted plants can also work here. They can watch you plant, care for, water, weed, and collect flowers or vegetables for your table.

Materials: A child-size watering can or mister, half-full of water; a small basket to collect flowers or vegetables (optional)

PEDAGOGY:

1. Bring your child to your garden, or area of potted plants.
2. Model how to walk around and touch the plants, describing and naming them.
3. Invite your child to touch the plants gently. Explain that you have to water the plants because plants drink water.

4. Give your child the watering can and ask them if they would like to water the plants. Show them how you hold it with two hands. Then, have them pick up the can with two hands: "See how easy it is to do with two hands not just one?"
5. If available, have them pick any vegetables that are ready for harvest and put them in a basket to carry inside for dinner.
6. Remember to let them explore.

Montessori Extension: For those without a garden, growing plants in a window box is a great alternative. You might even give your child their own plant to care for and watch grow.

Let's Move!

Given your toddler's newfound mobility, they'll need safe spaces where they can move about and explore. During this second year, take them to a playground, ideally one designed specifically for toddlers. Help them navigate and explore the structures and let them climb. Go for nature walks and watch them become more balanced as they maneuver over unpaved surfaces. And always let them walk as much as possible.

Your toddler's proclivity for movement goes beyond walking. It involves large and small muscles that need exercise. Take the pillows off the couch and set up an indoor obstacle course. Let your child run, jump, climb, and swing.

Smaller muscles in the fingers and tongue require particular attention during this year, too. Let your little one dig into sand, soil, Playdough—anything that works those fingers. Have them exercise their mouth muscles by blowing bubbles (see page 71). Balls are an endless source of fascination and fun, providing opportunities to throw, catch, roll, kick, and more. Just make sure your environment is prepared to handle the wayward ball.

In this section, I've provided some ideas to get you and your toddler started. But let your imagination run wild. Take stock of your space, indoors and out, and see what additional activities you can come up with to encourage your child's movement.

Montessori Says:
A child who has become master of his acts through long and repeated exercises, and who has been encouraged by the pleasant and interesting activities in which he has been engaged is a child filled with health and joy and remarkable for his calmness and discipline.
—*The Discovery of the Child*

ACTIVITY #1
Let's Walk Like a Cat!

Description: Through observation, your child has seen how other humans—and animals—move their bodies. In this activity, you'll use those observations to help them discover new and different ways to move their own.

Materials: None needed

PEDAGOGY:

1. With your child, watch how a cat moves, either via video or in real life (if you happen to have a cat). Point out the cat's movements to your child: "Look how it's crouching down. Look how it jumps up."
2. Ask your child: "Can you move just like the cat?"
3. Show them how the cat moves, perhaps by crouching down and jumping up yourself. (You'll want to tailor these movements based on your child's age and physical ability.)
4. Establish a clear starting point and end point for you and your child to move the way the cat does: "Let's stand here by the couch and go all the way to the kitchen like the cat does."

Montessori Extension: Try moving like other animals your child has seen in nature or in your home or read about in books. Then, ask them to make the sounds the animals make, as well.

ACTIVITY #2
Let's Push, Pull, and Lift!

Description: Children need lots of exercise to develop their muscles. These activities will provide exercise and also help your child practice their balance because of the different materials stored in the jugs.

Materials: Two empty 1-gallon jugs with handles and lids (clear ones work best), water, feathers, food coloring, glue, floor tape

PEDAGOGY:

1. Thoroughly rinse the jugs. Fill up one of the jugs halfway with water and add the food coloring. Fill the second jug with feathers, also halfway.
2. Put the caps back on and glue the lids in place.
3. Place both jugs next to your child. Then walk to the other side of the room.
4. Ask your child to bring you the jug with the feathers. When they've done so, ask them to bring you the jug with the water. Allow your child to bring the jugs to you however they wish—lifting, pushing, or pulling—until they get used to handling them. Comment on what you observe: "Wow, that water is heavy." "The feathers are lighter, easier to carry."
5. Next, place a six-foot-long line of tape on the floor. Model walking on the line while holding one of the containers.
6. Invite your child to do the same.

Montessori Extension: Be mindful of the weight. Fill the water jug with less water if you think your child will be more successful. Vary the materials you place in the jugs—flower petals, shredded paper, sand—starting off with the lightweight materials. Replace the straight tape line with a zigzag.

ACTIVITY #3
Let's Paint!

Description: The sweeping arm movements involved in painting help your child develop important muscles while being creative at the same time. This activity shows children proper finger grips, and how to control the amount of water on a brush. They also get to see the effect their brush strokes have on paper. Once they show control over their movements and an ability to keep the water on the paper, you can introduce chalk or crayons.

Materials: Paintbrushes, butcher's paper, tape, container filled with ½ inch of water

PEDAGOGY:

1. Tape about three feet of butcher's paper to the floor.
2. Place the container of water in the middle of the paper.
3. Model picking up the brush, placing it in the water, and "painting" on the brown paper.
4. Hand the brush to your child and let them try. Let them use whichever hand they like and encourage large strokes of the arms.
5. If the paper does not get too saturated, roll it up when dry for future painting sessions.

Montessori Extension: Tape the butcher's paper to the wall and allow your child to see what gravity does to the paint and water.

Let's Express Ourselves!

Montessori learned that if a child did not develop language within their first few years of life, it was usually much harder to acquire it later. Infants and toddlers are unconsciously learning how to understand what you're saying; they're developing their "receptive language" skills. During this time, children can understand 10 times more than they are able to verbally express.

Continue to fill your child's world with language but be more intentional. During their second year, children will unconsciously absorb your grammar and syntax, so use them correctly. For example, say "What would you like?" instead of "What does baby want?"

You can help your children understand the wonderful rhymes and rhythms of language by repeating the same songs and poems. Families who have the good fortune of being bilingual should speak both languages at home. Likewise, make a habit of telling family stories and encourage different family members to share their tales.

As part of their social and emotional development, toddlers begin to hear not only the words but also the tone in which words are spoken. Make a conscious effort to express how you're feeling in words.

With a greater capacity for language, comes a greater capacity for creative expression. Make up silly songs with lots of repetition to sing with your child. And tell them silly stories. Do, however, let them know that these songs and stories are silly. Children are still learning the difference between reality and fantasy.

Montessori Says:

Montessori saw a child's simultaneous linguistic and physical development as part of nature's grand plan. "So man develops by stages, and the freedom he enjoys comes from these steps towards independence taken in turn. . . . Truly it is nature which affords the child the opportunity to grow; it is nature which bestows independence upon him and guides him to success in achieving his freedom," she writes in *The Absorbent Mind.*

ACTIVITY #1
Let's Read Stories!

Description: From birth on, you have been introducing your infant to simple board books with one picture or word per page. Now, your one-year-old is ready to hear short, simple stories that have a beginning, middle, and end. Books with rhythm and rhymes are wonderful choices at this age.

Materials: A beginner storybook (see Resources, page 134, for ideas)

PEDAGOGY:

1. Invite your child to sit on your lap and look at a book with you.
2. Show them the cover and tell them the title.
3. Model how to turn the pages as you read.
4. Stop to ask questions or make observations before turning each page. Model reading to your child, as well. Show them the pages and let them see all the letters so they begin to understand that words are extracted from symbols.
5. If your child says "again" when you finish a story, read it again. Reading the same story over and over builds order and engages the child's memory.
6. Ask them questions about the book: "Did you like all of the dogs in that book?"
7. Place the book back where it belongs. Some, such as sturdy board books, should be available for your child to look at any time. Others, usually those with paper pages, are special, and should only be read with an adult until they're older.

Montessori Extension: Children love to look at pictures of themselves or familiar objects. Create a photo book with pictures of your child, family, and familiar places to "read" to your child.

The book should have about five pages and have one theme, for example, headshots of family members, or photos of animals, snacks, or your child's toys. Five 4- or 5-inch-square photos of the same category.

ACTIVITY #2
Let's Go to the Store!

Description: Children love to ask questions, but they should also be *asked* questions and allowed to come up with answers. In general, you should begin with simple questions that have a "yes" or "no" response. Then move on to questions that elicit another one-word response. The grocery store provides ample opportunities to ask questions and expose your child to useful vocabulary words.

Materials: None needed.

PEDAGOGY:

1. Invite your toddler to go to the store with you. Explain to them why you're going: "We are going to the store to buy fruit."
2. As you travel down the aisles, observe your child and follow their gaze. See what captures their attention. Stop to talk to them to confirm what they are looking at: "Do you see all of these bananas?" "Should we buy some bananas to bring home?"
3. Move on to the next aisle and engage them some more: "Do you like apples?"
4. Explain the origins of the food: "The apples come from apple trees. The farmer picked them, and the delivery person drove them here to the store so that we can buy them and bring them home for a snack." Give your child lots of vocabulary even if they cannot repeat or recall the names of the fruit this time.
5. Continue choosing items, asking your child questions, and providing answers.

Montessori Extension: Engage in this activity when you go to the beach, the park, the post office, and so on. Share the wonder of the world with your child.

ACTIVITY #3
Let's Shake Things Up!

Description: This activity is a great way to introduce children to music, while also refining their sense of hearing, balance, and creativity. You can make your own shaker by putting some rice, pebbles, or sand in a container and a secure lid.

Materials: A variety of shakers, basket, rhythmic music, a music player

PEDAGOGY:

1. Place a variety of shakers, such as rattles or maracas, in a basket.
2. Take a shaker out, hold it up to your right ear and shake it, and then hold it up to year left ear and shake it again. Then, place it back in the basket.
3. Repeat with each shaker until all of the them have been shaken and heard.
4. Ask your child if they would like to try shaking the instruments near their ears.
5. Finally, put on some rhythmic music and shake the instrument along to the beat. Invite your child to shake along.
6. Try exposing your child to many types of music. Observe what they seem to enjoy. Tell them the names of the genres, artists, and songs.

Montessori Extension: Encourage your child to dance and sing along to the music while shaking their instrument. Dancing is a great way to help your child express themselves, while moving their body in new and exciting ways.

Before You Move On . . .

Looking back on this past year, you'll be amazed to see how much your child has grown. They have progressed from holding on to things to stand, to toddling, to being able to walk. From gestures and cries, they've begun to use words to communicate. And instead of you always feeding them and changing their diapers, they are now beginning to prepare snacks and use the potty—although not always successfully!

The next year holds many more, equally exciting developments for your child. They will continue to forge ahead in their sensitive periods for mobility, language, and sensory experiences, while exhibiting an ever-greater desire for independence. This is a wonderful stage in your child's life. Here are a few things to keep in mind as your child moves into their third year:

- A two-year-old child moves much faster than a one-year-old child. You'll continually need to rethink your environment through their eyes.

- Two-year-olds have boundless energy. Plan for movement activities, inside and outside of your home. In addition to their large muscles—legs, arms, and torso—you'll need to prepare some activities for their fingers, toes, tongue, and nose, as well.

- Watch out for signs of frustration in the coming year. Two-year-olds are prone to meltdowns due to the influx of new information and their striving for independence.

- Congratulate yourself on your fundamental role in your child's growth. Certainly finding the energy and patience can be stressful at times, but raising a child is also the most rewarding experience there is.

Chapter

5

Entering Early Childhood: The Third Year

Now your child is moving into their third year of life, you will see them developing into an independent being right before your eyes. Their physical agility, verbal skills, and social tendencies grow their self-confidence and independence. In this chapter, I focus on how to handle the explosions of emotions—also known as tantrums—and new developmentally appropriate activities for your growing child.

Encouraging Independence

All children undergo transitional times in their lives. The first is birth, when they move from the attachment of the womb to functioning in the outside world, becoming independent human beings who are nonetheless still dependent on their mother.

A second transition period begins around 24 months, during your child's third year. At this point, your child realizes they can walk away from you, express themselves both verbally and nonverbally, and control what goes in and comes out of their bodies. Adults are still making a majority of the decisions for them, of course, but they are beginning to make choices of their own. During this year, you'll likely see a major boost in your child's independence.

Rather than stifle this independence, Montessori's philosophy encourages it. To Montessori, it was critical to foster independence and use it to facilitate other areas of your child's development—physical, social, emotional, and cognitive. In this chapter, you'll discover how to nurture your child's burgeoning sense of self through careful observation, a newly prepared environment, giving choices, and redirecting behavior.

Keep in Mind

Here are a few things to keep in mind as you read this chapter and implement Montessori's teachings into your child's third year of life.

Independence is a good thing, but you are still in charge. You design the environment, provide the materials, and set the limits. Your child will find security, stability, and order in knowing you are the stable anchor in their life.

Have patience. This new sense of independence will create some occasionally trying situations between you and your child.

Continue to observe your child. See what your child sees, hear what they hear, taste what they taste. Be amazed by all that they are taking into their unconscious mind.

Plan for physical activity (see page 93). Two-year-olds want to (and should) move quite a lot. Once a child can walk, they should be encouraged to do so as much as possible.

It's time to really let your child lead. Redefine the amount of autonomy you can give to your child at this stage. Their freedom during this year helps them develop independence and confidence.

Choices let you control the outcomes. Choice is a win-win for you and your child. They get to choose, and you always offer two choices that both work for you.

Make your home friendly for this age. This way, you can control what your child has access to, while giving them a sense of freedom.

This period will go by in the blink of an eye. Enjoy and cherish it.

Your Child's Development

You may have heard about the "terrible twos," but, in fact, there is no such thing. Two-year-olds are incredibly inquisitive, delightful, and full of energy and a love for life. As they begin their third year of life your child will amaze you with all that they do each and every day.

PHYSICALLY. Your child is very active this year. They will be going up and down stairs, walking backward and sideways, hopping, throwing and kicking balls, turning doorknobs, building block towers, using crayons, and solving puzzles. You may notice a preference for them to use their right or left hand. As your child continues through this period of sensory development, you'll want to continue to give them as many experiences as possible.

Let them taste ingredients before they are combined and then after they are mixed or heated. Have a listening session and introduce different kinds of music. Have a "touch bin" filled with items with interesting surfaces such as seashells, pompoms, mud, or snow. Ask them to describe what they feel and help them if they don't have the vocabulary.

EMOTIONALLY. Independence is a predominant feature of a child's third year of life. As their independence grows, they'll experience pride, confidence, and higher self-esteem. Your child is working on their self-control, moving from aggressive behavior toward more constructive actions. They will become accepting of redirection.

SOCIALLY. Your child will become increasingly self-aware, seeing themselves as an individual separate from others but will remain egocentric. They will understand and express "me" and "mine," as they demonstrate a shift toward independence.

COGNITIVELY. Language explodes this year. Your child will be able to name body parts and label toys. They'll also start using pronouns, plurals, past tense, and verbs, combining words to form sentences, expressing their ideas and thoughts with the acquisition of up to 1,000 new words.

MORALLY. Your child is picking up the mores of your home and family. They are learning about the food you prepare, the language(s) you speak, and the holidays you celebrate.

The Prepared Environment

A two-year-old's inquisitiveness is full speed ahead. Now that they're capable of moving around with greater ease, they have a growing curiosity about the world around them. There are so many tasks, objects, and wonders you can introduce them to. Near your front door or the foyer, consider adding a hook for their backpack and a mirror so they can see themselves before leaving home. In the kitchen, they'll become eager to help you prepare meals, set the table, serve the food, and clean up. If you have a garden, take a look around and see which child-size tools they are now able to handle. Remember to follow their lead—and capitalize on their independence to help them learn and grow.

THE BEDROOM

Every child needs their own space, whether it's half of a shared bedroom or a bedroom of their own. Their own space allows them to keep their possessions with the assurance that they will not be disturbed by others.

Additionally, each child requires their own sense of identity. Even if your child is sharing a bedroom with siblings or other relatives, giving their space its own identity is important. Children at age two can distinguish between colors, so let your child pick their favorite, and use it to define their area, the storage units, and the bedding. Consider painting the walls and furniture the same color as well. If it suits the room, add an area rug and curtains in the same tone.

To be clear, you don't need a massive amount of space for your child to feel independent. All they need is to feel that it is *their* space.

THE PLAY SPACE

In this third year, you'll want to make changes to your child's play space that reflect and facilitate their growing sense of self, muscle development, socialization, creative expression, and more.

You can start with the walls. Add a child-size mirror where your child can see their reflection and make faces to express various emotions. Hang a small chalkboard or a large magnetic board with magnetized shapes and letters (to prevent choking, make sure they're too big to fit inside a toilet paper roll).

To help your child exercise those small finger muscles, attach a four-foot-long string to the wall and add clothespins for hanging art or attach felt shapes. To boost their vocabulary and sense of place, collect photos of pets, family, friends, nature, animals, and the like. Hang them on the wall.

Add some puzzles with about four or five knobbed pieces to your child's shelves. Also add a basket with multi-itemed sets, such as DUPLO sets. Observe your child to see which materials they use most, rotating out the ones not used with something new.

This is the year you'll want to engage your child in the kitchen even more than before. Add a step stool so they can have access to some safe counterspace. Invite them to join you in your food prep, identifying each ingredient and allowing them to mix, spread, shake, and taste. Leave the exact number of place mats and napkins needed for the next family meal on an accessible shelf and have them set the table before meals. Let your child help wipe off the table after the dishes and utensils have been removed, and put the sponge back at the sink.

THE BATHROOM

If they haven't already, children at this age will start to use the toilet (see page 68 for more on potty training). In the beginning phases, it's still a good idea to remind them throughout the day: "Do you need to stop and check your body? Think and see if it feels like you need to go to the bathroom."

Continue to dress your child in clothes they can easily remove to use the toilet such as pants with elastic waistbands. Place a step stool next to the toilet, if needed. It's easier for a child to pull a tissue from a box than to use toilet paper. After using the toilet, have them get in the habit of "flush and wash." If they cannot reach the sink, have that step stool available.

At this age, bath time gives your child a chance to show you how much they can do. They can remove their clothes, place them in the hamper, get in and out of the tub themselves (always with your supervision) and run the washcloth over their own bodies. They are also able to put all of their bath toys back in the mesh bag.

It might be fun, on some days, to put your child in a bathing suit, give them a sponge and child-friendly foaming bubble spray, and let them wash down the walls of the tub. They love helping out—and this is a playful way for them to do that.

Tantrums and the "Terrible Twos"

Your two-year-old's brain is developing at an incredible pace. They can now understand hundreds of words and sentences, but they're only able to express a tenth of what they know. For example, they may be tired and hungry from their constant movement, but be unable to share this with you. At the same time, they are increasingly aware that others are moving their bodies in ways they'd like to move theirs but have not yet mastered.

This combination of factors would be frustrating for anyone, so just imagine how frustrating it is for your two-year-old. As a result, your child may experience tantrums, flailing about, hitting and throwing things, crying, screaming, or banging their head. This is the body's way of letting out a lot of pent-up energy very quickly. Once a tantrum starts, the child is out of control, so you'll need to make sure they are in a safe place and out of the way of others. Be near them, but do not touch them. Acknowledge their experience: "I see you are upset. I am here for you when you feel better and gain control." If the tantrum happens in public, try to ignore the glares of people around you and remove your feelings from the equation.

Though it may seem like these meltdowns last forever, they generally subside in a matter of minutes. When your child has gained control, acknowledge it: "I see that you feel better now. Would you like some water?" Afterward, you can talk about it: "How did that feel when you could not control your screaming? Was it scary?"

To avoid tantrums, get to know your child's tolerance level for various things. Reflect on past tantrums to identify potential triggers. Do they need time to change from one activity to another? Are they simply hungry or tired?

Remember: Tantrums are a natural phase of child development. Your child is developing cognitively at a much faster pace than they are emotionally and linguistically. It will all balance out eventually.

Let's Explore!

Your two-year-old will likely want to go everywhere that they can see. So, ensure what they see is as appealing as possible.

Exploration at this stage also occurs in the social world. Now that they understand more words and are more easily expressing their desires and ideas, they will also begin to understand what boundaries are and begin to negotiate with the adults around them.

Montessori developed a series of didactic materials to help three- to six-year-olds learn through their senses. Though she was only able to work with children three years and older, she realized from her studies that there were sensitive periods for development that began at birth.

Modern Montessori preschool programs have adapted this philosophy and designed attractive and safe materials for children from birth to age three. These materials encourage age-appropriate touching, tasting, smelling, and listening. (See Resources, page 134, for examples.)

If your child likes to place objects in any place they seem to fit, then it is time for some activities that lets them do more of that. You can use existing Montessori activities or create some of your own. For example, take an empty coffee canister and make a one-inch slit opening on top. Give your child five wooden tongue depressors or Popsicle sticks and have them put the depressors/sticks through the slits, counting as they do. Color the sticks and slits and have the child match them up when sorting.

You already fill your child's life with sensorial experiences. Now just be more mindful of them and give them the vocabulary to go with the experiences.

Montessori Says:
The environment must be rich in motives which lend interest to activity and invite the child to conduct his own experiences. —*The Absorbent Mind*

ACTIVITY #1
Let's Match the Smells!

Description: The sense of smell is of great interest to young children. In this activity, you will make your child aware that there are many different scents, scents have names, and scents can be matched. This builds vocabulary and refines the sense of smell.

Materials: Four small, opaque containers with holes on top such as empty spice jars, two different-colored permanent markers, lemon rinds, freshly grated nutmeg, a place mat, basket

PEDAGOGY:

1. Fill two containers with the nutmeg and two with lemon rinds.
2. Mark the bottom of the two nutmeg containers with one color, and the bottom of the two lemon rind containers with a different color.
3. Place the four containers inside a basket, along with the place mat.
4. Invite your child to work with the materials in the basket.

5. Lay the place mat on the table, take out one container at random, bring it up to your nose and smell it, exaggerating the act so it's obvious to your child what you're doing. Do the same with the three remaining containers. Then, put them back in the basket.

6. Next, select just two containers, smelling one and then the other. Have your child smell one then the other. Ask, "Do they smell the same or different?"

7. If they say "the same," turn the containers upside down to see if the colors match.

8. If they don't say "the same," put one container away. Then, choose another from the basket, have your child smell it, and continue until they identify two that smell the same.

Montessori Extension: Using nontoxic products, change up the scents inside the containers. Try cinnamon or dried oregano. When your child masters this activity with four containers, add one more set of scents.

ACTIVITY #2
Let's Take a Nature Walk!

Description: When you take a child for nature walk, they are using their senses of smell, vision, hearing, and touch to experience things that are not in your home. They are experiencing a natural world with no artificial or plastic materials. There are many things to absorb and wonder about. They can feel the weather. They see the world and its creatures and plants and start to develop empathy for their environment.

Materials: Basket for collecting things

PEDAGOGY:

1. Take your child on a walk on a nature path. Encourage them to notice their sensory experiences: "Let's stop, close our eyes and listen." "What did you hear?" What do you smell? "Shall we touch the soft ferns?"

2. Collect leaves, twigs, rocks, and burrs to take home in your basket. "Let's find five big pine cones. Now let's find five small pine cones." "Let's find some flat round rocks."
3. Take photos to remember your trip and to talk about later.

Montessori Extension: Children love the sensorial experience of playing in a puddle of water or mud. Let them enjoy it. Just remember to bring wipes and hand sanitizer to clean up afterward.

ACTIVITY #3
What Do We See?

Description: Children love to look at things. Looking at things through a magnifying glass, seeing the details bigger, is better. It makes them wonder how it is that things look bigger through a glass.

Materials: Plastic magnifying glass

PEDAGOGY:

1. When out for your nature walk, point out an ant on the ground. "Look at the ant. It is small and hard to see. Look at this special glass that makes things look bigger. It is called a magnifying glass. Let's look at the ant through the glass."
2. Show your child how to hold the magnifying glass and see the ant appear larger.
3. Look around for other things that your child can view, such as a leaf or a pine cone.

Montessori Extension: Have a basket of things to look at through the magnifying glass in your home and switch out the items regularly: seashells, flowers, yarn, loose tea leaves.

Let Me Do It Myself!

Independence is the most notable aspect of your toddler's development this year. They have learned enough language by now to indicate refusal or say, "I can do it myself." Try not to make this an issue. Power struggles can be avoided by restructuring what is available for your child to choose from: Would they like toast or a muffin for breakfast, a banana or an apple for a snack?

With the Montessori method, children are encouraged to complete tasks by themselves, thereby building confidence and self-esteem. The more they can do on their own, such as brushing their hair or dressing themselves, the more willing they'll be to stick with a challenging activity or task until they master it.

There are many practical life activities around your home that your child might be able to accomplish, if they are broken into child-size chunks. For example, helping to carry in the groceries, or helping to fold the towels. These activities, which require repetition, exactness, and perfection, give your child some feeling of control over the order in your home. In the following section, I'll provide a few more ideas to get you started.

Montessori Says:
Education must begin at birth.
—*1946 London Lectures*

Montessori continually spoke of the impact that childhood has on the future individual. Adults don't just happen—they are the result of experiences that the child was presented.

ACTIVITY #1
Let's Use a Sponge!

Description: In this activity, children transfer water from one container to another using a sponge. This develops hand-eye coordination, concentration, and self-esteem. Once they've mastered the concept of left to right they can begin transfering with utensils and then from container to container. All of these practical life activities promote small muscle development and a sense of accomplishment. Also, learning to move things from left to right is a prereading and writing practice.

Materials: A sponge, water, two identical bowls, a tray, small square of paper towel

PEDAGOGY:

1. Fill one of the bowls with water, about three-quarters of the way to the top. Then, place both bowls on a tray—the one with water to your child's left and the empty one to their right—with a sponge in the middle and the paper towel on the side.
2. Sit next to your child, and, using two hands, pick up the sponge and place it in the bowl full of water. Then, lift up the sponge and squeeze the water out over the other bowl.
3. Invite your child to try. "Would you like to try? Both hands. Does the water feel wet or dry? Let's move all of the water from the left bowl to the right bowl. Squeeze."
4. Have them continue to do this until all of the water in the left bowl is gone, at which point you can say, "Empty."
5. Then, turn the tray around so that the bowl full of water is once again on the left side of your child, and perform the activity again. Dab up any spilled water with the paper towel.
6. Return the materials for this activity to a place your child can find them next time.

Montessori Extension: Try using food coloring in the bowl with water. This will make it easier to see where the water is. Replenish the water daily or more often so that it is always fresh and inviting.

ACTIVITY #2
Let's Hang Up Our Clothes!

Description: This activity assists in small muscle development. The tension of clothespins varies, so test them out first to ensure they'll be easy for your child to manipulate. If you have an outside clothesline your child is familiar with, explain that the clothesline in this activity is just for them.

Materials: Four feet of yarn, tacks, 10 clothespins, two matching baskets, 10 infant- or child-size socks

PEDAGOGY:

1. Find a place in your child's play area to attach the yarn with tacks at each end to form a clothesline. Make sure it's in easy reach for your child.
2. Put the clothespins in one basket and the socks in the other and place them near the clothesline.
3. Invite your child to try this activity.
4. Show your child how a clothespin works. Take one out of the basket, hold it up, and pinch the end: "Do you see? When I pinch here the other end opens." Repeat this a few times.
5. Then, place the open end of the clothespin on the yarn and let go. Repeat with all 10 clothespins, until your child has mastered both opening them and attaching them to the yarn.
6. Show your child how the socks can be attached to the clothesline with the clothespins. Invite them to try and practice.
7. When finished, place all of the socks back in one basket and all of the clothespins in the other.

Montessori Extension: If your child has difficulty placing the clothespins on the line, have them place the clothespins around the edge of a bowl instead. You want them to be successful, so be mindful of making activities easier. You can also cut out felt shapes, letters, and numbers for your child to attach.

ACTIVITY #3
Let's Pour!

Description: In addition to developing small muscles and improving concentration, these tasks bring children a sense of pride and mastery. The skills they're developing will aid them when they are helping to prepare family meals, pouring their own cereal and milk (and possibly yours), and helping to feed your pets. In this activity, children pour from left to right.

Materials: A tray with two small matching child-size pitchers (creamer-size), sand, a child-size whisk, a hand sweeper

PEDAGOGY:

1. Fill one pitcher with sand (about half way to the top)
   - Place a tray in front of your child.
   - Place the pitcher with sand on left side of the tray and empty pitcher on the right side.
   - Invite the child to the activity.
   - Make sure the child is pouring from left to right.
2. Pick up the sand-filled pitcher with two hands, one on the handle and one underneath.
3. Pour the sand into the second pitcher, then put down the empty pitcher.
4. Invite your child to try.
5. Have them continue to pour from one pitcher to the other.
6. When your child is finished, show them where the materials will be kept for them to use again.

Montessori Extension: Once your child has mastered pouring dry materials, move on to water. Fill the pitcher about halfway up with water. Provide a sponge so the child can wipe up any spills. Some people add blue food coloring to the water to make it more visible.

ACTIVITY #4
Let's Comb Our Hair!

Description: Learning to take care of ourselves is important at all ages. Your child has learned how to dress themselves, brush their teeth, and feed themselves, and now will learn to adjust their hair. This gives them a sense of control over their appearance, pride in doing it themselves, confidence, and independence.

Materials: A mirror placed at child's level on a tabletop or wall, a comb and/or a brush in a basket close by

PEDAGOGY:

1. Show your child the mirror and comb/brush set. "I see you in the mirror. Where is your hair? Let's see what happens to your hair when we comb/brush it."
2. Model how the comb is to be held and how it goes through the hair.
3. Note how brushing and combing changes your child's hair: "See? Now, your hair is all going the same way."
4. Place the brush or comb back in the basket.

Montessori Extension: You can also use this setup to teach your child other things, like applying lip balm or sunblock.

ACTIVITY #5
Let's Clean the Vegetables!

Description: Caring for their family's home environment lets children feel that they are making a contribution. They learn how to do something by themselves that helps the group. When they complete this activity, they also see the wonder of the transformation of soil-covered food to a clean edible vegetable. This is the groundwork for nutritious, healthy eating.

Materials: A few small vegetables from the garden, farmers' market, or grocery store, such as carrots that your child can easily hold, a bowl that will fit the carrots, a tray, water, vegetable brush

PEDAGOGY:

1. Put some water in the bowl.
2. On the tray, place a carrot, the vegetable brush, and the bowl of water.
3. Show your child the tray and talk about the carrot. For example: "This carrot came out of the ground at the farm. We need to clean it up so we can eat it for dinner."
4. Dip the brush in the water and hold the carrot with one hand and with the other dip the brush in the water. Demonstrate how to clean the carrot.
5. When finished, put the brush down and watch your child's reaction to seeing the clean carrot.
6. Let your child try. If they don't have a dominant hand, let them decide which hand should hold the brush.
7. When finished, show your child where the clean carrot should go in the kitchen and thank them for helping prepare dinner.

Montessori Extension: Your child can help clean a variety of vegetables before dinner. This will also encourage them to eat more vegetables.

ACTIVITY #6
Let's Take Care of Our Pets!

Description: Take advantage of your child's powerful drive to do things themselves at this age. Let them help take care of the others in your home. Feeding the pets builds empathy toward other creatures in addition to letting your child feel independent, useful, and confident in successfully doing things themselves.

Materials: Your dog's feeding bowls, scoop, pitcher of water, sponge, tabletop hand broom, used-dish bin

PEDAGOGY:

1. Talk about being hungry and eating and how your pets get hungry and need to eat, as well.
2. Show your child where the dog's food is and how to scoop out one serving and put it into the food dish. This should be on a low, accessible shelf.
3. Show your child where the pitcher of water for the dog is and how to pour it into the dog's water bowl, and then place the pitcher in the used-dish bin.
4. Allow your child to wipe up any spilled water and replace the sponge.
5. Allow your child to sweep up any spilled dry food and put in the trash.

Montessori Extension: Do the same procedure for the cat, rabbit, or whatever other pets you have in your home. Eventually your child can help clean the bird's cage or the fish tank. If you have no pets, then let your child be responsible for watering or misting certain plants.

Let's Move!

Your child is growing quickly and working hard to master the coordination of their muscles and limbs, both large and small. Don't be afraid to present them with some challenges—their quest for independence will drive them to meet them.

In particular, your yard, or any safe outdoor space you have access to on a frequent basis, provides a wealth of opportunities for your child to move around this year. Tree stumps are great for stepping onto, hopping off of, and jumping over. Low (very low) trees are great for branch-swinging and hanging. Mud is great for sliding around in and trying to maintain one's balance.

You might also consider incorporating some activities outside of the home, such as swimming lessons and toddler gym programs, which provide a safe space for the kind of climbing, sliding, jumping, and playing that most homes just can't accommodate.

Don't forget the smaller muscles. This year, help them learn to use utensils, crayons, scissors, buttons, zippers, and the like. Continue to engage your child in Playdough, DUPLO, knobbed puzzles, finger (or toe) painting, and fat crayons. Also let them engage in practical life activities that involve finger movement, such as shucking corn, eating with chopsticks, or helping you knead dough. Expose your child to musical instruments such as keyboards. To improve the muscles in their mouths, recite poetry, sing songs, and practice tongue twisters.

Montessori Says:
The child's individual liberty must be so guided that through his activity he may arrive at independence . . . The child who does not do, does not know how to do.
—*The Montessori Method*

ACTIVITY #1
Let's Go on an Adventure!

Description: This activity lets them move their muscles in novel, creative ways, gaining the coordination and self-confidence needed for independence. And they really have fun. Observe which movements your child enjoys and which they need more practice with.

Materials: Bedsheets and/or blankets, large pillows and/or couch cushions, cones or tape, Hula-Hoops, a play tunnel (optional)

PEDAGOGY:

1. Declare to your child that today is an adventure day, and you'll be moving your bodies in new and different ways.

2. Using chairs, couch cushions, blankets, bedsheets, and a play tunnel (optional), create an obstacle course in your play area. Use cones or tape to mark the starting and end points.

3. Make sure to incorporate various kinds of movements. Start by having your child crawl through the tunnel. Place lines of tape on the ground for your child to slide through. Make a ramp out of a couch cushion for them to use to roll down onto a pile of blankets.

4. Once they have the course down and have gone though it a few times, ask your child to go through it moving like a tiger, dog, frog, or bird, etc.

5. Repeat until your child is tired and then acknowledge their accomplishment.

Montessori Extension: Try creating an obstacle course outside, incorporating various aspects of nature.

ACTIVITY #2
Let's Move to the Music!

Description: Moving to music or dancing engages the child's sense of hearing, as well as their physical muscles. Children refine their sense of hearing by listening for the music to start and stop and creatively interpreting the sounds. They also gain more control over their body's movements. Make sure you offer this activity when your child is full of energy, not when they might be tired or approaching nap time.

Materials: A music player

PEDAGOGY:

1. Put on the music of your choice and encourage your child to move particular parts of their body: "Let's have our fingers dance." "Let's have our feet dance." "Can we make our whole body move to the music?" Model each suggestion.

2. Alter the music between slow and fast tunes. Encourage your child to move accordingly: "Does the music feel slow or fast?" "Can we move our legs slowly like the music?"
3. Then, switch between louder and softer music, and observe how your child alters their movement by volume: "Can you move your eyes softly?" "Let me see your arms moving loudly."
4. Think of all the movements a body can make and ask your child to move to the music accordingly.

Montessori Extension: Start and stop the music and ask your child to stop moving when the music stops and start again when it begins again. This encourages listening closely to the music, rather than getting carried away in the movements.

ACTIVITY #3
Let's Open Things Up!

Description: Children love to open things themselves, and they need to develop their small muscles to do so. This activity can be made more challenging as they master the original containers you put in the basket. This helps develop the small muscles and the skills necessary to master the buttons, buckles, and ties of their future clothing.

Materials: A basket; a solid-color place mat; five small containers your child can open and then close, such as a small coin purse with a zipper, a container with a twist-off lid, a small wallet with a snap, an eyeglass holder with a Velcro closure, an empty wipes container that opens and closes

PEDAGOGY:

1. Take the basket off of the shelf and say, "Look what I would like to show you."
2. Put the place mat on the floor. Take out one of the containers, carefully look at it and open it. Show your child it is open and say "open" and place it on the mat in front of you.
3. Open each of the five containers, saying "open" each time.

4. When all five have been opened, pick each one up in turn, close it, and say "close."
5. Invite your child to play. They may need help with some of the items. Show them. Help them. Scaffold them.
6. When finished, show them where the activity will be kept on the shelf.

Montessori Extension: Change out the containers as you observe that your child can master them and is no longer interested in the challenge. Replace them with different containers, gradually increasing in difficulty.

Let's Express Ourselves!

Your newly independent child is starting to use their language to help them be understood and gain a foothold in the world.

At this age, your child's vocabulary is expanding by hundreds of words per week. Additionally, they have a stronger grasp on what a story is, so continue adding simple storybooks to your collection (or borrowing them from the library). Montessori believed that the more of a child's senses we engage during the acquisition of knowledge, the greater their understanding will be. So, for example, try incorporating finger plays and other movements into story time.

Paramount to language development is memory, so continue playing games that strengthen your child's memory. For example, have your child try to recognize and then recall the names of people from photos and animals from books you've read to them.

As your child's ability to express their thoughts improves, asking them questions and respecting what they have to say will boost their self-esteem, confidence, and independence. Moreover, questioning invites wonder, which invites creativity and ignites the imagination. Imagination is an important aspect of your child's being able to reach their full potential.

Children this age are acquiring the ability to use crayons, paint, clay, and musical instruments. When they present you with what they have "drawn," it's important to comment on it objectively: "I see you made some red lines." If you say how much you like it, the child may be inclined to make things for your pleasure. Praise the effort, not the product.

> ### Montessori Says:
> The adults in the child's world are there to set up an inviting environment which piques the child's curiosity and interest. This is also true of the arts. "The teacher's task is not to talk," Montessori wrote in *The Absorbent Mind*, "but to prepare and arrange a series of motives for cultural activity in a special environment made for the child."

ACTIVITY #1
Let's Perform a Finger Play!

Description: Finger plays are a great activity for children. They address their tendencies for communication, repetition, perfection, and activity. They expand vocabulary and memory skills. Memory is very important, as it is needed for speaking, reading, math, and science as they grow older.

Materials: A list of finger plays is helpful if you do not know them off the top of your head. You'll find many books with these in your local library and on the Internet.

PEDAGOGY:

1. Sit and face your child.
2. When you have their attention start your finger play.
3. Say the following words and model the gestures:
   - "Open." Open your hands with the palms facing your child.
   - "Close." Close your hands into a fist.

- "Open, close." Open your hands and then close them into a fist.
- "Give a little clap." Clap twice.
- "Open, close." Open your hands and then close them into a fist.
- "Put them in your lap." Move them to your lap.
- "Creep them, crawl them, right up to your chin." Move both of your hands up to your chin.
- "Open wide your little mouth." Slowly open your mouth.
- "But do not put them in." Quickly move your hands behind your back.

4. Repeat periodically over the next few days until your child has the words and the actions memorized and becomes an enthusiastic participant.

Montessori Extension: There are many finger plays to choose from, such as "Five Little Pumpkins," "Itsy Bitsy Spider," and "Wheels on the Bus."

ACTIVITY #2
Let's Recite Poetry!

Description: Poetry invites creativity, imagination, music, memory, and messages into language. Reciting poetry gives a child pleasure as the words rolls off their tongue. It instills confidence when a child has memorized a poem. In addition to the classic children's poems, there are many poems that families often pass down from their cultural heritage. You can also make up poems and use poetry time to observe how your child is developing rhyming and rhythms.

Materials: A collection of poems

PEDAGOGY:

1. At a calm, quiet time of day, sit down and face your child.
2. Recite a short, simple poem that has rhythm and rhyme. Make sure it's one you know by heart and really like. Your child will pick up on your enthusiasm.

3. For example, "Who has seen the wind? Neither you nor I, but when the trees bow down their heads, the wind is passing by."
4. You may move parts of your body or gesture along with the words. This helps your child remember the poem.
5. Then try funny poems: "I eat my peas with honey. I've done it all my life. It makes my peas taste funny. But it keeps them on my knife."
6. Repeat these and add more until your child knows a repertoire of poems by heart.

Montessori Extension: Other classic poems for children include the Mother Goose poems "Hey! Diddle Diddle," "Humpty Dumpty," "Baa Baa Black Sheep," "Mary Had a Little Lamb," "This Little Piggy," "Hickory Dickory Dock," "Little Boy Blue," and "Rub-a-Dub-Dub, Three Men in a Tub." There are dozens available online and in children's libraries and bookstores. (See Resources, page 134.)

Telling jokes serves a similar purpose to reciting poems. Start with simple jokes, with a repeatable format, such as: "Why did the chicken cross the road? To get to the other side." "Why did the cow cross the road? To get to the other side." "Why did the monkey cross the road? To get to the other side." See how many animals your child can come up with.

ACTIVITY #3
Let's Make a Book!

Description: Your child is well aware of books by now. They will be moving on to reading books themselves in the next few years. As they get closer to 36 months, it is a good time to let them know about the concept of writing a book. The written word is another form of expression. All children like to write their own books.

Materials: Five 4-by-6-inch pieces of white paper, two 4-by-6-inch pieces of card stock or construction paper, stapler or other fastener, crayons or markers

PEDAGOGY:

1. Introduce the idea of making a book: "Would you like to make a book about colors? What color crayons should we use?"
2. Have them pick out three to five crayons. "Thank you. I see you picked yellow, blue, orange, and red. What do you want to draw?"
3. Give the child a piece of white paper and ask them to pick one crayon and then let them draw whatever they wish. When they are finished, put the paper aside and take out another piece of blank paper.
4. Ask: "What color should we put on this paper? And what do you want to draw?"
5. Continue to provide the child with blank paper and crayons until all are used.
6. Then, attach the papers together, use the card stock to create front and back covers, and write your child's name on the front cover.
7. Then ask: "What should the title of this book be?"
8. Write the title that your child suggests on the cover.
9. Read the book together and put it on the shelf with the other books.

Montessori Extension: The types of books your child could make are endless. For example, they could paste in photos of people, animals, and trips, or draw shapes and flowers. The important thing is that they realize that they can express themselves in this format and that their book is respected and valued.

ACTIVITY #4
Let's Ask Questions!

Description: Asking questions to make a child wonder is an activity for adults to engage in to foster their child's thinking skills.

Materials: None

PEDAGOGY:

1. Be observant and see what your child is looking at and might be thinking. Ask questions about it. "Why is that bee going from flower to flower?"

2. Ask "why" questions. "Why does your cereal get soggy when the milk is in it for a while?"

3. Do the third part of the three-point lesson (page 35) with names of things you know that they know. "What color is this shirt?" "What shape is this?"

4. Ask questions that involve memory. These should be about events that happened in the past—recently or long ago. For example, at night you could ask: "What did we have for lunch today?"

5. Ask them "who" questions. For example, if they're looking at photos, ask, "Who is this person?"

6. Ask "where" questions, such as, "Where should this toy go?" or "Where do we go to get more milk?"

7. Ask "how" questions, such as, "How did the cat get on top of the table?"

8. Don't ask "when" questions yet. They come at a later developmental stage.

9. Just ask a few questions over the course of the day. Don't overwhelm them.

Montessori Extension: Extend this method of communication to other family members, as well. It will work wonders in improving relationships between adults, which is all the better for the child's environment.

Before You Move On . . .

This past year, you have watched your toddler develop into a walking, talking individual who has started to exert their independence. Here are a few points to consider as you move on to the next year of your child's life:

- Your little one will continue to assert their independence (a sensitive period for this) with more and more attempts to do things on their own. They will be able and willing to do many things with their improved dexterity and with the help of the activities and environment that you have prepared.

- Your child has started to use language (another sensitive period at this age) and has become quite social this past year. As they move into their next year, they will acquire more language and become more aware of social interactions. As they approach their third birthday, they will move from parallel playing into more interactive play with their peers. They will build on the emotional traits of empathy as they interact and become more aware of their peers.

- Sensory development is still important, as your child is still in the sensitive period for this. Having them engage in activities that help them refine their five senses continues to be important. Learning to discern the difference and similarities in the things they see and hear, will help with the beginnings of reading.

- Children will move from playing with blocks as blocks to having them represent other things. Creativity will blossom, especially since you have been laying the foundation of confidence in expressing their ideas.

- Movement will become more refined and toileting will be mastered in the next phase of your child's development.

Looking Ahead: Ages Three to Six

Your infant has quickly grown into a two-year-old. They are now entering the magical age of childhood where they will see, absorb, and express the wonders about them with the boundless energy to capture it all. They are developing socially and gaining independence, yet they still circle around you, their center of gravity. They are becoming the adults that they will someday be.

Preparing for the Years to Come

Maria Montessori designed the original Casa dei Bambini and all of its materials for this age group. From ages three to six, children typically become much more interested in other children. At this stage, when children have gained a stronger sense of self and others, as well as a greater capacity to communicate, they will now begin to interact with one another. Preschool, especially, offers them the opportunity to engage with their peers—not to mention, gives them access to a wealth of materials unavailable at home.

Going forward, you'll notice further attempts at independence—so be ready to prepare your home accordingly. Perhaps one of the most exciting changes involves your child's ability to perceive objects as representative of other objects. When a block can become a car or a rocket ship, your child's imagination becomes boundless. Moreover, it's this same development—seeing objects as symbols—that allows them to perceive letters as representatives of sounds to be written and read, and numbers as representatives of quantities that can be added and subtracted.

Of course, during these three years your child will be moving into a mixed-age program of children from three to six years of age. This is because they are entering a different stage of socialization where they become less egocentric and start to engage with other children in the environment. In this chapter, I'll provide some advice on preparing for school—both Montessori and not—as well as a more detailed snapshot of their incredible development from ages three to six.

Preparing Your Child for School (at Home)

One of the most significant changes to occur this year may be the start of preschool or moving from an infant/toddler/two program to a preschool of three-to-five-year-olds. Your child has been developing independence with you at home (or in their childcare facility). They are becoming less egocentric and more interested in other children especially ones a bit older than themselves.

Montessori had a three-year age span in her rooms. It reflected reality. Younger children like to learn from older children and older children like to reinforce their knowledge and gain confidence and self-esteem in that relationship. Having a three-year age span allows children with the same level of functioning in say math or language or reading to work together, regardless of age.

The most important thing about having your child start school is that you must be ready to separate from the child. You must be willing to give your child to another adult. If you're excited to start this new chapter, then your child will be excited, as well. Your child will pick up on any hesitation you have about this.

If your child has difficulty separating, see if they can go for a shorter period in the beginning. Most schools have a phase-in schedule that allows for the child and the parent to feel comfortable with the separation. Have your child go for the last hour, and then build up to going for the last two hours and so on.

As the first day of school approaches, use a calendar (a month-by-month calendar that hangs on the wall) to get your child ready for preschool. Mark the first day and mark the days they'll be in school.

SET UP PLAYDATES WITH FUTURE CLASSMATES. When they do start, it is comforting to see familiar faces and to feel welcomed by new "friends."

WALK OR DRIVE BY THE SCHOOL. Take the same route to familiarize your child with the routine, just as you will when school starts.

ADD A FAMILY PHOTO TO YOUR CHILD'S BACKPACK. Seeing you will provide them with a sense of comfort in their new environment.

LET THEM BRING A BLANKIE OR SECURITY ITEM. If your child has one, you might cut and hem it so a small piece fits in their pocket. Reaching in to hold it gives them comfort when they may not be allowed to bring in the whole blanket.

PLAN A SPECIAL ACTIVITY TO CELEBRATE THE FIRST DAY OF SCHOOL. Do something different and unique to mark this significant day, like going for ice cream or to a park you don't always go to.

SHOW YOUR CHILD WHERE THEY CAN HANG THEIR NEW BACK-PACK. Also let them know where their school work will be kept.

ASK YOUR CHILD WHICH SNACKS OR LUNCHES THEY'D LIKE FOR SCHOOL. Remember to add something special to their lunch box, such as a heart or smiley face drawn on a napkin. On the first day have them help you prepare it.

BUY A HAT OR T-SHIRT THAT REPRESENT YOUR CHILD'S SCHOOL. You and your child can wear it around town. This helps them build a sense of pride and identity with their school.

"SHOULD I SEND MY CHILD TO A MONTESSORI SCHOOL?"

Children of all ages, backgrounds, and abilities are welcome in Montessori classrooms. Maria Montessori embraced the world's diversity and encouraged children in the social study and geography curriculums to find wonder in the people of the world.

Montessori schools have a wealth of materials and space to set them into various areas for practical life, sensory experience, math, language, writing, geography, social studies, and art. While Montessori programs have these activities available, their focus is on individual socialization skills.

Montessori is not a licensed or copyrighted term, so when you're researching a Montessori school, confirm that they're credentialed in a program. Any school can say they are Montessori-based, but if they have been credentialed you know that the teachers have been trained and have continued professional development.

Montessori schools exist in a variety of options. There are Montessori charter schools that are free and Montessori public school options that are also free. Montessori schools may be nonprofit and run by religious organizations or nonprofit boards of parents. These schools tend to give tuition aid. Some Montessori schools are run for profit and may consist of one room or a network of schools. Montessori schools can also be found in people's homes. Certified Montessori Teachers sometimes choose to set up their own programs at home for a group of children. Montessori programs generally separate children into groups younger and older than three years of age or at 18 months depending on local licensing regulations.

You should also consider the logistics of the school you choose for your child. Think of the location of the school. How will it work into your commute? How convenient is it for playdates after school? Another issue is cost: Take a thoughtful look at your budget and be realistic about what you can afford, if the school isn't free.

Whatever school you choose, you must feel comfortable in it and know that your child will be, as well. Children attending Montessori preschools do quite well in both progressive and traditional kindergartens. Montessori children have formed a love of learning, independence, concentration, and self-esteem that serves them well wherever they go.

IF YOU'RE PLANNING ON SENDING YOUR CHILD TO A MONTESSORI SCHOOL . . .

Most Montessori schools have an orientation session, where you'll meet with the school's staff and your child's teachers. Typically, you'll be asked to share some information on what's been happening at home, languages spoken at home, what your expectations are for your child when they start school, and your reasons for choosing Montessori. The teachers will likely offer some suggestions as to what you should do or not do at home, now that your child is starting school.

If you are planning to send your child to a Montessori school, it is best to wait and let the school introduce them to the classic didactic Montessori materials such as the pink tower, the brown stairs, and the red and blue rods. You don't want to confuse your child by having them use the material one way at home and another way at school. The Montessori teachers will decide when to introduce a given material in an exciting way.

Remember that children take a while to adjust to school. At first, the staff will see to it that your child is adjusting, both socially and emotionally. Because Montessori teachers tend to let the child lead, you might have to be patient, reset your expectations, and allow your child some time before they dive into the more cognitive, academic areas of school. Montessori teachers partner with families and other professionals to decide the best ways for your child to achieve their potential.

IF YOU'RE *NOT* PLANNING ON SENDING YOUR CHILD TO A MONTESSORI SCHOOL . . .

Should you decide not to send your child to a Montessori school you can still use Montessori as your guide during your free time and at home.

From age three on, your child is in a sensitive period for socialization (see page 11), becoming less egocentric and more willing to communicate with others. If you're waiting another year to send them to preschool, it's still a good idea to arrange playdates with other children. Socializing with peers helps develop empathy, problem solving, and leadership skills.

While at home, you can continue to encourage independence by leveling up your child's practical life activities. Have your child help wash the car, fold the laundry, feed the pets, water the plants and garden. Almost anything that needs to be done, you can teach them how to do, provided they're enjoying it and the activity is safe.

As you prepare for them to enter kindergarten, ask the principal or teachers about the school educational philosophy to see if it aligns with what you're teaching your child. If the school uses the kindergarten year to learn and say, the sound of letters and identifying numbers, you could choose to spend time cooking, pottery, or stargazing. Think outside of the box. Take your child on trips to the art museum, zoos, and for hikes. Introduce them to cuisines and cultures from around the world. Continue to ask thought-provoking questions and to give your children freedom with limits.

Should you decide to send your child to a traditional preschool program where your child isn't given the freedom of movement that they're used to, be sure to explain that there are different rules in the new school. Continue to give your child a sense of control and confidence at home. Most children are like dandelions—they can grow anywhere. Others are like orchids and need a special kind of school environment. You will be able to differentiate this by observing your child or getting feedback from professionals.

Your Child's Development

Up until now, your child has unconsciously absorbed an incredible wealth of information about the world around them. They've learned to speak your language(s), move their bodies about, and mimic your activities; they've even begun to embody your culture and mores. As your child continues to unconsciously absorb the intricacies of social interactions, physical movement, and more, they'll also start to seek out certain experiences and information. This is the fundamental difference between the *unconscious* absorbent mind and the *conscious* absorbent mind. The transition marks the second half of the first plane of development Montessori outlined. The next plane is from ages six to 12, when your child enters a more sensitive period for mental independence and a strong sense of moral order, fairness, and justice.

Consequently, the next three years will see your child become a social animal, speaking more clearly, in full sentences, and with an expanded vocabulary and understanding of the rules of grammar. They will be able to follow multiple-step directions. They will play pretend and will learn to distinguish between fantasy and reality. They will tell stories, recite memorized poems and songs, begin to understand time. They grow from understanding "before" and "after" and the sequencing of events to understanding the *concept* of time, and be able to anticipate events. They will show affection and empathy while learning how to take turns, and separate more easily from their parents. Ultimately, your child's desire to do things for themselves will help them further master their world physically.

That said, Montessori was aware that progress does not always move in one direction. Children learn in fits and starts; oftentimes, they'll take two steps forward, one step back. Your child may be toilet trained, for example, but after a few weeks have a number of accidents that require wearing a diaper before they're ready to try again.

In the pages to follow, I'll highlight several key areas of their development, within the context of Montessori's pedagogy. Regardless, by the time your child turns six, they will have moved from a dependent infant to an independent child.

SENSORY AWARENESS

From infancy to age three, your child was unconsciously absorbing information through their senses. From ages three to six years, they will actively, consciously seek out information to refine their senses and develop the capacity to describe what they're seeing, hearing, tasting, touching, and smelling.

Montessori showed us how to isolate each sense so that children can define their unique qualities. Each of the sensorial materials she designed emphasizes one defining quality, such as color, weight, texture, size, sound, taste, shape, or smell. One example is her pink tower: a series of 10 pink cubes, the first of which is one cubic centimeter, the second of which is two cubic centimeters, and so on and so forth. A child can stack the cubes or lay them down in a row from largest to smallest, they can see the gradation of size and feel the gradation of weight, and make adjustments when they're incorrect. Critically, all of the blocks are the same material, texture, shape, and color, making the only differentiating factor their volume.

Montessori classrooms are full of these materials, but you can achieve the same effect outside of school. Walk around your house, stop in a room, close your eyes for a few moments, and ask them to describe the smell: "How does the bedroom smell different from the bathroom or basement?" Take a stroll around the neighborhood and prompt them to notice the scents of various restaurants—a bakery, a pizzeria, a BBQ, etc. Make your child more aware of their senses and give them the necessary vocabulary to identify what they're experiencing.

In particular, continue to spend time in nature—whatever that means for you and where you live. You'll find many textures, sights and sounds to experience and identify. If you have the space, plant a herb or vegetable garden. Children love to prepare the food they are eating and learn where the food comes from. The magic of mixing and/or heating ingredients is the beginning of scientific inquiry in chemistry. Continue cooking with your child, expanding to other cuisines from different areas of the United States and the world.

The more different ways in which a child takes in information, the easier it is for them to learn, remember, and incorporate that information into other ideas. By touching and feeling cubes, letters, and amounts, a child understands them at a different level than if they had just heard about them or seen them. This is why Maria Montessori designed her didactic materials.

> **Montessori Says:**
> The senses, being explorers of the world, open the way to knowledge. Our apparatus for educating the senses offers the child a key to guide his explorations of the world. —*The Absorbent Mind*
>
> The hand is the instrument of intelligence. The child needs to manipulate objects and to gain experience by touching and handling. —1946 London Lectures

READING AND WRITING

Since birth, your child has absorbed your language and all its vocabulary. They began to speak, expand receptive and expressive language, and refine their auditory and visual discrimination senses. Once a child can distinguish between and isolate sounds, they move on to recognizing the letters. When a child sees and remembers that the letter "m" represents the sound "mmmmm" and the letter "o" represents the sound "ooooo," they're soon introduced to putting them together, in order to read the word "mom." Montessori introduces the lowercase letters by their sounds and the uppercase letters by their names. This is a pre-reading memory activity.

Some children start to have this auditory discrimination at age three, and others do not master it until age five. Children need this auditory discrimination to be taught to read phonetically. Some children learn to read via visual memory. They are told and see the word, identify the word, and can recall its definition. This is referred to as sight reading. Some children can do both. All children have different learning styles.

Montessori's introduction to writing starts with children acquiring the pincer grip by using crayons and paintbrushes. They then work on controlling their hand movements with the metal insets. They also trace letters with their fingers, made out of sandpaper, usually mounted on boards. Children trace letters with their fingers to feel the patterns. They then trace or write the letter for which they know the associated sound to form words that they are starting to read phonetically. Children learning to read through visual memory will write the whole word from memory. If you recall, they have also been using materials from left to right to get them used to moving from left to right as they read and write. These are the sensitive periods for reading and writing that Montessori talked about, from about ages four and a half to six.

Once the children learn the relationship between the sounds and the letters, they have the knowledge to read and write many words. Details are the result of other peoples' investigations and designs. Knowledge is having the ability to investigate and make your own designs. Give children knowledge and you give them the power to keep learning. See what they do with it.

Montessori Says:
Here is an essential principal of education: to teach details is to bring confusion; to establish the relationship between things is to bring knowledge. —*Childhood to Adolescence*

MATH

From the time your child was an infant, you have been practicing rote counting with them—the memory skill that's foundational for mathematical work. This includes the memory skill of learning the names of the symbols ("two" is the word for "2"). Showing them objects one at a time so they understand is called one-to-one correspondence. Children come to understand one-to-one correspondence at different ages—some around age three, some not until age six. They need this concept to start addition and subtraction.

Typically, Montessori teachers also observe children to see if they have developed "conservation of matter." In other words: Do they realize a cookie broken in half is still one cookie? Or do they think that as a result they now have two cookies? Some children come to the correct conclusion closer to five years of age.

Regardless, children during this age range become intrigued with numbers and quantities. Once your child can rote count, recognize numbers, and understand one-to-one correspondence and conservation of matter, they can further their math concepts by manipulating Montessori didactic materials. They manipulate chips, counting one to one, match them to the number symbol, and see the difference between different numbers. Montessori is also known for her golden beads that children use to see large quantities. Her materials are designed on the metric system so children are exposed to that form of measurement in addition to the American method with inches, feet, ounces, and pints.

A fun activity for children is to have them count a bucket of seashells by counting them from one to 10 and, each time they get to 10, they put a pebble in their pocket. When they are all counted, they count by 10s for each pebble and then add on any left over. This is the base-10 system at work.

Montessori Says:
Children display a universal love of mathematics, which
is par excellence the science of precision, order, and
intelligence. —*Maria Montessori: Her Life and Work*

PRACTICAL LIFE AND SELF-CARE

Your child has been gradually given the opportunity to do things for
themselves and build up their confidence and self-esteem. With more
guidance and a prepared environment, they can master a surpris-
ing number of tasks. They are able to help wash your car, tend the
garden, sweep pathways, rake leaves, and shovel snow outside. Inside,
they can organize and clean their rooms, help with meal preparation,
set the table, and clean up. They help dress themselves and their
younger siblings and take care of the plants and animals in your
home. They will carry things for you and straighten up the house
when asked. You may still give them two choices, but as they age,
they make decisions knowing what the expectations of the family are.

Most have learned how to get themselves out of bed, pull up
and straighten their bedcovers, choose one of the two outfits left
out for them, take off their pajamas and put them under their
pillow, dress themselves, go to the bathroom, wash their face and
hands, brush their teeth, comb their hair, and be ready for the day
and to tackle more challenging tasks.

If the environment is set up to allow for this freedom of movement,
children in this age range can learn to set the table for breakfast, pour
their cereal and milk, feed themselves, and clean up. They can also do
this for a sibling or their parents—almost like breakfast in bed.

Once they get used to going to school, children like to and are able
to pack their own lunches, put on their shoes, and get ready for the
day. Once you put them in the car, they can learn to buckle their own
car seats (if you go by bike, they can likely put on their own helmet).

In the kitchen, utensils are great for small muscle development.
Moreover, this is the age where the transformation from numerous ingredients to a finished dish is magical, sparking a child's

imagination and interest in math, science, and technology. Picky eaters are also more likely to eat things that they have prepared.

At bedtime, your child can help bathe themselves, brush their teeth, put their worn clothes in the hamper, and pick out a book to read.

> **Montessori Says:**
> When it comes to practical life activities and tasks in particular, it's best to let them master the activities on their own and feel the satisfaction that comes with that achievement. "The fundamental help in development, especially with little children of three years of age, is not to interfere," Montessori wrote in *The Child, Society, and the World*. "Interference stops activity and stops concentration."

ART AND SCIENCE

In their first few years of life, your child has been exposed to and absorbed works of art from around the world, at different points in history. Children from ages three to six are incredibly creative. They enjoy the sensorial experiences of art—the process of making it, if not the finished product.

Additionally, they have seen the beauty of their own prepared environment, in the form of the various artworks, furniture, and photographs as well as books, in your own home. Now, they have the dexterity, confidence, and concentration to use the materials to create pieces of art themselves with crayons, markers, chalk, paintbrushes, scissors, paint, glue, glitter, clay, watercolors, and more. Once they have learned the craft of how to use various media, they are then able to create their own art. Children ages three to six can be brought to museums and they are able to identify styles of art like pointillism, impressionism, and contemporary.

From the time they were infants, you have been singing to them and exposing them to music, songs, and instruments of different genres and cultures. Perhaps they've even been making up their own songs. During this stage, you can both enjoy the creations that they come up with.

There are some programs that teach children how to use various musical instruments. If your child shows interest in learning how to play an instrument, and loves it, great. It has to be fun.

In general, wonders surround children at this age—from watching a plant grow to creating their own dance moves, imitating animals, or watching a bowl of ingredients turn into something entirely new and delicious. This abundance of wonder is to be nurtured and encouraged throughout their life. Montessori wanted children to have the freedom and the confidence to explore their environment and, ultimately, create a better world.

Feel the music . . . feel the satisfaction of a job well done . . . feel the ease and peace of what you have accomplished in providing opportunities for your child at whatever their abilities may be.

Montessori Says:

The satisfaction which they find in their work has given them a grace and ease like that which comes from music. —*The Discovery of the Child*

Resources

Organizations
American Montessori Society
Association Montessori International
The Montessori Foundation
Zero to Three

Websites
amshq.org
cdc.gov > ncbddd > childdevelopment
cdc.gov > nutrition > foods-and-drinks > choking
dailymontessori.com
Facebook: Montessori Toddlers
montessori.org
MontessoriGuide.org
themultilingualhome.com

Movies/DVDs
Babies
Edison's Day

Materials
Montikids
Nienhuis Montessori

Books for parents
Maria Montessori: Her Life and Work by E. M. Standing
The Absorbent Mind by Maria Montessori

The Discovery of the Child by Maria Montessori
The Montessori Method by Maria Montessori
The Secret of Childhood by Maria Montessori
The Six Stages of Parenthood by Ellen Galinsky

Books for the first year
Baby: Colors! by DK Publishing
Baby Faces by Margaret Miller
First Words by Roger Priddy
Mother Goose by Gyo Fujikawa
See, Touch, Feel by Roger Priddy

Books for the second year
Brown Bear, Brown Bear, What Do You See? by Bill Martin Jr. and Eric Carle
Chicka Chicka Boom Boom by Bill Martin Jr. and John Archambault
Click, Clack, Moo: Cows that Type by Doreen Cronin
This Is a Book of Shapes by Kenneth Kraegel
The Very Hungry Caterpillar by Eric Carle

Books for the third year
The Cat in the Hat by Dr. Seuss
Freight Train by Donald Crews
Goodnight Moon by Margaret Wise Brown
If You Give a Mouse a Cookie by Laura Numeroff
Where the Wild Things Are by Maurice Sendak
The Wonderful Things You Will Be by Emily Winfield Martin

References

American Academy of Pediatrics. Media and Children Communication Tool Kit. Accessed November 11, 2020. https://www.aap.org/en-us/advocacy-and-policy/aap-health-initiatives/Pages/Media-and-Children.aspx.

American Academy of Pediatrics. Where We Stand: Screen Time. Accessed November 11, 2020. https://healthy children.org/English/family-life/Media/Pages/Where-We-Stand-TV-Viewing-Time.aspx.

Cohen, Danielle. Why Kids Need to Spend Time in Nature. Accessed November 11, 2020. https://childmind.org/article/why-kids-need-to-spend-time-in-nature.

Hill, David L. Why to Avoid TV for Infant and Toddlers. Accessed November 11, 2020. https://healthychildren.org/English/family-life/Media/Pages/Why-to-Avoid-TV-Before-Age-2.aspx.

Monroe, Martha C., and Kristen Poppell. Why Is Exposure to Nature Important in Early Childhood? Accessed November 11, 2020. https://edis.ifas.ufl.edu/fr394.

Montessori Life. Accessed November 11, 2020. https://amshq.org/Educators/Membership/Montessori-Life.

Montessori, Maria. *The Absorbent Mind*. Holt Paperbacks, 1995.

Montessori, Maria. *The Child in the Family*. ABC-CLIO, 1989.

Montessori, Maria. *Education for a New World*. ABC-CLIO, 1989.

National Center for Montessori in the Public Sector. Growth of Public Montessori in the United States: 1975 to 2014. Accessed November 11, 2020. https://public-montessori .org/white-papers/growth-of-public-montessori-in-the -united-states-1975-2014.

Zero to Three. What Are The Most Important Changes in the Brain After Birth? Accessed November 11, 2020. https://www.zerotothree.org/resources/1379-what-are -the-most-important-changes-in-the-brain-after-birth.

Index

Acknowledgments

Where would I be without my cohort of Montessorians—Mimi Basso, Karen Deinzer, and Maria Gravel, my three cofounders of the Montessori Infant Toddler Teacher Training Program at WSMS-TEP? We have been colleagues and friends for more than 100 years, known one another's families, and taught one another's children and each other. Thank you for all your support, sharing your wisdom, our adventures in China, millions of laughs, and for sharing this wonderful life.

About the Author

 **Tara Greaney, MS,** has more than 40 years of experience in early childhood education, and this is her fifth academic year as head of school at Morningside Montessori School, New York City. She previously established the Cravath Children's Center, the first corporate childcare center in New York City, and served for 27 years as its Director. Prior to that, she was Director of the Early Program at The Caedmon School on Manhattan's Upper East Side, which was the first Montessori school in New York City. Tara is one of the founding faculty members of the Infant Toddler Montessori teacher training program at the West Side Montessori School Teacher Education Program (WSMS-TEP). She has taught at WSMS-TEP for six years in New York, and also taught Montessori courses for multiple summers abroad in China. She holds AMS teaching credentials at both the Early Childhood and Infant/Toddler levels, and earned her MS in Educational Leadership from Bank Street College. Tara's writing has been published in *The Parents' & Teachers' Guide to Helping Young Children Learn*, as well as *The Review*, the annual publication of the Parents League of New York. She has presented workshops on various topics related to Montessori education and child development. Tara has traveled extensively around the world and resides in New York City and Naples, Florida. Her best experience ever is being a parent, to Michael.

CPSIA information can be obtained
at www.ICGtesting.com
Printed in the USA
BVHW050608040622
637825BV00003B/13